100
WAYS
TO BE
KIND

BOOKS BY THERESA CHEUNG

The Sensitive Soul

Dream Dictionary A to Z
21 Rituals to Change Your Life
The Premonition Code
21 Rituals to Ignite Your Intuition
Answers from Heaven
An Angel Called My Name
The Ten Secrets of Heaven
The Afterlife Is Real
The Moon Fix
The Birthday Encyclopedia

100 WAYS TO BE KIND

THERESA CHEUNG

Thread

Published by Thread in 2020

An imprint of Storyfire Ltd.
Carmelite House
50 Victoria Embankment
London EC4Y 0DZ

www.thread-books.com

ISBN: 978-1-80019-091-7
eBook ISBN: 978-1-80019-090-0

The information contained in this book is not advice and the
method may not be suitable for everyone to follow. This book is not
intended to replace the services of trained professionals or to be a
substitute for medical advice. You are advised to consult a doctor on
any matters relating to your health, and in particular on any matters
that may require diagnosis or medical attention.

Kindness should become the natural way of life, not the exception. Buddha

CONTENTS

PREFACE

A NEW WAY OF LIVING

Kindness is the force, the power the world urgently needs right now to reinvent itself. The global pandemic and the senseless injustice that triggered a wave of Black Lives Matter protests signal as never before the need for a new way of living. As well as offering a simple guide to making kindness not just something you do but your new way of life, this book offers evidence to prove that kindness truly is the best and only way forward for you, the people you care about and the world to heal.

If I told you that acts of everyday kindness can boost your mood and immunity, lower blood pressure, ease anxiety, make you look and feel younger, improve all your relationships (including the one you have with yourself) and give you a sense of deep meaning and purpose, you would probably think this all sounds too good to be true.

But it isn't!

Often the simplest solutions are the best ones. Kindness is the simple and scientifically proven remedy that you and everyone on the planet urgently need to administer right now.

So, if you want to find your meaning and purpose and help save, connect and heal the world at the same time, but aren't quite sure how – as the pre-virus, pre-Black Lives Matter era tended to marginalise the drive within us all to be kind – this book is for you and your brave, beautiful new life and world.

CHAPTER 1

INTRODUCTION

Rebuilding a life of meaning and purpose

The Coronavirus made its presence felt around the time I started work in earnest on this book. I was totally immersed in gathering lots of proven-to-be-good-for-you ways to be kind. In recent years, it has felt as if many of us have forgotten how to be kind or simply don't know where to start, so the book was going to offer a road map of practical and simple ways to be kind, encouraging you to commit to the 100 days of kindness challenge.

My sincere desire to write the book was further heightened when, just as I was starting to write the first few sections, news of the heart-breaking suicide of a famous TV star broke. What made it so poignant and relevant was that her final Instagram post read: 'In a world where you can be anything, be kind.' This lady seemed to have it all, but having it all when you can't see or feel kindness in your life feels as if you have nothing. Her story is not an isolated one. Ask any Samaritans volunteer who mans the helpline. They will tell you that loneliness and the feeling that no one in the world cares about you is lethal.

None of my initial intentions for this book have changed. It will still offer all that, and more. But what has undoubtedly changed is the world itself. Out of nowhere came the pandemic, and its life-changing impact slowly but surely became horrifically clear to everyone. Then in the midst of all this our collective hearts were broken yet again by the events that triggered a wave of the Black Lives Matter protests. Not to take these massive shifts into account when writing this book would be incongruous.

The Coronavirus has thrown everything we think we know about our lives and what really matters up in the air. The Black Lives Matter movement has forced us all to take a long hard look at ourselves and our unconscious prejudices. Our daily routines have changed completely, and even when the world returns to normal – which it eventually will – things will never be quite the same again, not least because of the risk of further outbreaks or different viruses but also because there is a long road ahead to ensure the world becomes a place of true justice and equality for all people.

Ignoring these seismic global shifts would make this book feel out of touch instead of a life-changing guide to finding meaning and hope, and changing your life for the better, as I had always hoped it would be. For example, some of the ways to be kind I was originally going to suggest – such as a warm, firm handshake – simply may not be possible or safe until there is an effective, proven vaccine for Coronavirus. Watching the world crumble, my motivation to write the book as originally intended collapsed. It felt meaningless, so instead of bashing away, I decided to put it aside and come back to it, focusing my energy on doing free online talks and offering my help and advice wherever I safely could.

Einstein famously said, 'We cannot solve our problems from the same level of thinking that created them.' What I needed to do was to change my thinking about the book and make it not just a treatise on the power of kindness to heal lives but rather something that clearly spoke to the present crisis and offered up a practical solution for rebuilding a life of true meaning and purpose during and after the pandemic. The minute I decided to do that, my motivation for the book came back in an instant. I couldn't wait to start writing it from scratch.

Then it struck me again. My decision to switch the focus to helping others had not only boosted my energy and mood, it had given me a sense of real purpose and made me feel so much stronger and better able to cope with the uncertainty. There *was* light at the end of the tunnel. With so much talk in the media about the crucial importance of finding a vaccine to immunise against the virus, and how to counter centuries of injustice and racism, I sensed that giving kindness the spotlight and offering a practical 'how-to' path towards this could be part of the healing solution.

Obviously, being kind can't actually stop someone getting the virus or repair broken systems based on racism and oppression. But what it can do is offer you a desperately needed sense of purpose, joy and hope during these uncertain times. If you have this inner strength, your chances of pulling through and emerging stronger from any struggle or setback that life throws at you dramatically increase. Contrary to what you may believe, it is not anger or aggression that bring out your true inner grit, but kindness. Kindness gives your life meaning.

Finding meaning

Many of my books deal with bereavement and finding meaning after the loss of a loved one. Perhaps you know the excoriating pain of grief following the death of someone in your life. Or perhaps you have not been able to say goodbye to loved ones – and my heart goes out to you. But whether or not you have lost someone close, you will be experiencing a bereavement of sorts. Why? Because bereavement is loss. It can be the loss of a loved one, but it can also be the loss of a relationship or a job ending or anything that makes you feel there is no going back.

We have all lost our old way of life and will therefore experience the five stages of grief psychologists[1] have identified – anger,

---

1 Kübler-Ross, E. (2007) *On Grief and Grieving: Finding Meaning through the Five Stages of Loss*. Scribner.

denial, bargaining, depression and acceptance. These stages don't always follow a set order – and everyone's journey through grief is unique – but we all experience the overwhelming trauma of the grieving process at some point and, sooner or later, we are all going to start accepting that we have to say goodbye to life as it was and accept this strange new world of hand-washing, social distancing and questioning of long-held beliefs. I believe, and state in many of my books, that there is yet another aspect of grief following acceptance, and that is finding deeper meaning. As the planet moves towards healing from the shock of the pandemic, and global acknowledgement of centuries of oppression and racial injustice, we are all being offered an unprecedented opportunity to reset our lives and find deeper meaning.

So, what is the deeper meaning?

We aren't going to know the answer to the big 'why' questions, like why bad things happen to good people. This life is rather like the underside of a tapestry – all confusing knots – but perhaps somewhere there is a beautiful picture that makes perfect sense. However, even if we aren't going to find out why, we must never stop *asking* why.

Imagine a world where we knew why bad things happened. Would we bother to be kind? We would likely become desensitised and apathetic. Asking why encourages us to be more compassionate and, every time we flex our compassion 'muscles', we grow emotionally and connect with what truly matters in our lives.

In recent years, it felt as if the balance of the world was tilting heavily towards the material. I often felt such despair. Increasingly, it seemed that being selfish and externally focused was the only way forward and that truth didn't matter any more, just spin. Injustice, excess, cruelty, lack of empathy and connection and unkindness abounded. Nobody wanted to listen or compromise. We were mistreating not just ourselves but others, animals and the planet itself. I sensed there had to be some kind of huge shift to tilt the world back towards something deeper and more meaningful. I just didn't think that shift would happen in my lifetime.

Think about it. The virus began with animals and spread from China, where so many of our material goods come from, and it thrives in urban centres where money talks and pollution levels are high. It has forced much of the population into a monastic, mindful existence in their homes. When venturing out now, you *have* to be kind and think of others and the impact of your actions. Again, this is opinion and not fact, but from my perspective our intolerable cruelty towards animals, our obsession with status and wealth, looks over personality, the death of empathy and our abuse of this beautiful world were increasingly dangerous threats to our holistic wellbeing. Genuine connection was withering. We were all social distancing long before it was government policy. If you went on a train, the Tube or a plane a few decades ago, people would look out of the window and perhaps talk to each other, but in the recent pre-virus world it was ear plugs in, heads down, scrolling through their phones. Was it high time for some kind of shift to propel us towards a kinder way?

Pollution levels are falling dramatically during the lockdowns. Kindness is trending online, with workers on the front line applauded instead of celebrities and reality TV participants. Newsfeeds have become more authentic, personal and meaningful and social media feeds are starting to become populated with role models for a life of integrity and purpose at long last.

A little anecdote… In the height of the lockdown, I went to the supermarket hoping to buy eggs. I couldn't locate them, so I asked the lady at the till. While I was asking her, a young boy went to the back of the shop, found the eggs for me and put them on the till without being asked. That would likely never have happened in pre-virus days and I thanked him for his kindness. The woman working in the shop commented that she was aware that people were being so much kinder to each other. She also said that while she hated the pain and anxiety of current times, for the first time in years she was enjoying her job again, because people noticed her and thanked her. It certainly gave me pause for thought. Has the virus made us kinder?

None of us is perfect and we have all been guilty of focusing too heavily on the material, valuing looks over substance and adopting a 'what's-in-it-for-me' approach to life, but what the virus has powerfully taught us is that meaning can never be found in status, wealth, popularity, relationships and external things – it has to be discovered within. It gave us no choice but to consider this inward-focused approach to life. To survive it, every one of us has had to look within themselves and consider what really matters and what we are doing with our one precious life. The Black Lives Matter movement gathering momentum during this time of global introspection has finally forced us all to acknowledge the underlying injustice and oppression in the world, and the false thinking of the 'other' as separate from us.

The events of 2020 are a giant wake-up call.

The fact that you are reading this book shows that you are ready and willing to answer that call. I could not be happier, because this is your moment.

I'm guessing a lot of you are compassionate, kind and gentle people who act with decency and love, and struggle to cope when confronted with injustice, cruelty and unkindness. You probably don't elbow your way through life or routinely put your needs above others. You likely don't judge people by their appearance, culture or race but see them for who they are – human beings just like you. You may also be comfortable with peace and solitude, needing it as a refuge from the overwhelming world. So, in many ways you are uniquely qualified to comfort, teach, lead and light up the way for others who may be struggling to adjust to the loss of external stimulation and all the changes the virus has forced into our lives.

As I have spent time in convent retreats and am an author who craves time alone and peace from an overwhelming noisy world, it's been revealing to find out that my preferred way of life is called quarantine. Joking aside, if you are someone who needs regular periods alone to recharge because you are sensitive, and if you have ever thought your empathy, inclusiveness and other sensitive traits are a weakness or that you don't fit into a world of extraverts, now is the time to recognise these traits for the strengths they are. Now is the time for your kindness and compassion to help heal and reconnect the world. All sensitive people[2] can help turn the tide and make the shattering of our collective hearts in 2020 a rebirth for the world – a compassion pandemic.

This will pass

The current crisis will eventually pass, just as the world wars, 9/11, Ebola, SARS (severe acute respiratory syndrome), bird flu and other man-made and natural disasters passed. The Black Lives Matter movement will become a significant turning point in history. It may take a while and the world may feel as if it is ending but, one day, we will return to our everyday lives. The important thing is *how* we return.

- Will we return with post-traumatic stress from our ordeal or with post-traumatic strength from our internal growth?
- Will we all return with an attitude of gratitude for everything we took for granted previously?
- Will we treasure the touch of a loved one?

---

2 Cheung, T. (2020) *The Sensitivity Code*. Thread.

- Will we value acts of everyday kindness?
- Will we emerge seeing the extraordinary in the ordinary?
- Will we retain the awareness that all our actions impact others and will we continue to think of their wellbeing?
- Will we focus on connection – the virus does not care what religion, culture or political persuasion someone is – rather than difference?
- Will we all emerge knowing that kindness and not self-ishness is our superpower?
- Will the key workers – doctors, nurses, carers, emergency service personnel, delivery drivers, shop assistants and many more – retain their current and well-earned status as true heroes?
- Will we judge people by who they are, rather than what they look like, where they come from or what they believe in?

In short, will we emerge deeper, wiser and kinder, more open-minded and tolerant people?

If we can emerge with post-traumatic strength and a sense of what truly is of value in our lives, we will have begun the most exciting journey of our lives – the journey to self-awareness and finding our meaning and purpose. I believe, in time, all of us will think of 2020 as a turning point; we will think of life in terms of before and after 2020.

I pray we seize the moment and make this a reset for ourselves and the planet. Every thought, feeling and act of kindness you now perform is a part of that reset. If you don't know where and how to start, you will find 100 empowering ways to kick-start your kindness in this book. Social distancing has been taken into account in outlining all of them.

Now is the time for every one of you to light the way and be the change you have always wanted to see in the world but thought could never happen. Well, it's happening right now. This is a period of global reflection as never before. Let's all emerge with greater self-wisdom, awareness of what truly matters, and less emphasis on the material and what separates us and more on kindness, interconnection, heart and soul.

And if you think you aren't ready to light up the way ahead – that in itself is a sign you are.

The science of kindness

Before we plunge into the ways to be kind and immediately start making a difference, I want to briefly draw your attention to the science of kindness. It's important for you to know at the outset that all the suggestions in this book are not anecdotal but backed up by solid research.

You probably already know that stress triggers the release of hormones that aren't good news for your wellbeing. Studies[3] show that stress hormones increase blood pressure, suppress the immune system and increase the likelihood of depression. What you may not know is that kindness also produces hormones and they have the opposite effect.[4] When you are kind or someone is kind to you, a hormone called oxytocin[5] is released, which lowers blood pressure and boosts immunity and mood. In short,[6] the kinder you are the more likely you are to experience happiness.

Another thing you may not know is that being kind can reshape your brain. Each moment you have an opportunity to rewire your

---

3 Guerra, A. *et al.* (2013) 'Clinical cardiology: Depression increases the risk for uncontrolled hypertension.' *Experimental and Clinical Cardiology*, Winter; 18(1) 10–12.

4 Raposa, E. *et al.* (2015) 'Prosocial behaviour mitigates negative effects of stress in everyday life.' *Clinical Psychological Science*, 4(4) 691.

5 Esch, T. *et al.* (2011) 'The neurobiological link between compassion and love.' *Medical Science Monitor*, 17(3) RA65–RA75. Published online 2011 March.

6 Otake, K. *et al.* (2006) 'Happy people become happier through kindness: A counting kindnesses intervention.' *Journal of Happiness Studies*, 7, 361–375.

brain by the choices you make, so your brain is constantly adapting and changing according to what you think, say and do every single day. Research[7] indicates that the more acts of compassion you perform, the more the areas of your brain associated with empathy are stimulated. Just as muscles need a workout to stay toned, so too does your brain. If you are constantly stressed all the time, the areas of your brain associated with stress will be strong, but if you choose to practise kindness instead, those stress areas will get weaker and your kindness 'muscles' stronger.

Even though it can seem otherwise, human beings are not born to be self-centred in a 'survival-of-the-fittest' world. In fact, we are born to be kind because, since humans first evolved (and research confirms this), children who are well looked after by their parents have stood a greater chance of surviving than those with uncaring parents. So, having kindness in our DNA is essential for survival and children born to parents who took good care of them are more likely to do the same with their own children, so the kindness gene is passed down the generations. In addition, communities that worked together in harmony and took care of each other, including the vulnerable, were also more likely to flourish. This is much the same way that communities that maintained peaceful relations with other communities were more likely to survive. Our ancestors had to learn to cooperate in order to survive within their own communities and with strangers, and humans with activated kindness genes had a much greater chance of this.

To cut an age-old story short, the kindness gene has stood the test of time and, even though it may be more developed[8] in

---

7 Engström, M. & Söderfeldt, B.A. (2008) 'Brain activation during compassion meditation.' PLOS ONE 3(3) e1897: *The Journal of Alternative and Complementary Medicine*, 2010, 16(5) 597.

8 Israel, S. *et al.* (2009) 'The oxytocin receptor contributes to prosocial fun allocations in the dictator game and the social orientations task.' PLOS ONE, 4(5) e5535.

some of us than others, it is present in us all. Kindness positively impacts our chances of survival, our health, our relationships and our wellbeing, and a lack of kindness has the opposite, detrimental effect on us and our children. So now you know about the kindness gene within us all waiting to be activated, what specific health benefits has science proved it can offer?

- Kindness helps us feel good about ourselves. Numerous studies[9] have confirmed that thinking of others or volunteering regularly makes people feel happier. It can also help ease depression,[10] as it seems that focusing less on ourselves, and more on the needs of others, makes people feel better.
- Kindness boosts immunity. Research suggests that when people watch or perform acts of kindness themselves, antibodies in the immune system indicating immune-system health increase significantly. This impact of kindness has been called the Mother Teresa effect – a study[11] showed that after students watched a film about the good deeds of Mother Teresa, their immune systems were strengthened.
- Kindness lowers blood pressure.[12] It appears that the kindness hormone, oxytocin, increases the production of substances in your bloodstream that can expand blood

---

9 Lyubomirsky, S. *et al.* (2004) 'Pursing sustained happiness through random acts of kindness and counting one's blessings: tests of two-week interventions.' Department of Psychology, University of California, Riverside.

10 Musick, M. *et al.* (2003) 'Volunteering and depression: the role of psychological and social resources in different age groups.' *Social Science and Medicine*, 56(2) 259.

11 McClelland, D.C. *et al.* (1988) 'The effect of motivational arousal through films on salivary immunoglobulin A.' *Psychology and Health*, 2(1) 31.

12 Jankowski, M. *et al.* (2016) 'Oxytocin and cardio-protection in diabetes and obesity.' *BMC Endocrine Disorders*, 16, 34.

vessels and help regulate blood pressure. This may explain why people in loving relationships often have healthier hearts[13] than those in relationships that are stressful.

- Kindness makes you look younger.[14] Stress is known to increase free radicals, (unstable molecules that can cause cell damage) which accelerate skin ageing, but when the kindness hormone oxytocin is released, free-radical damage is reduced significantly. In addition, because kindness also lowers blood pressure, more blood can reach the skin to flush out inflammation. In this light, you can think of kindness as natural botox for your skin.
- Kindness may improve your chances of gaining respect or positions of authority, in research[15] settings at least, where it has been shown that altruistic behaviour increases the likelihood of a person gaining positions of power in a group.
- Kindness improves the quality of close relationships and could well be the key to successful relationships.[16]

Myths about kindness

Science has proven that there are powerful, potentially life-saving, reasons to be kind. And the more science uncovers about the merits of kindness, the easier it becomes to debunk damaging myths.

---

13 Smith, T. *et al.* (2006) 'Marital conflict and coronary artery calcification.' American Psychosomatic Society's 64th Annual Meeting, Denver, CO, 3 March 2006.

14 Szeto, A. *et al.* (2008) 'Oxytocin attenuates NADP dependent superoxide activity and IL6 secretion in macrophages and vascular cells.' *American Journal of Endocrinology and Metabolism*, 2008, 295, E1495.

15 Hardy, C.L. *et al.* (2006) 'Nice guys finish first: The Competitive Altruism Hypothesis.' *Personality and Social Psychology Bulletin*, 32(10) 1402–1413.

16 Andersen, S.M. *et al.* (2008) 'Simple kindness can go a long way: Relationships, social identity, and engagement.' *Social Psychology*, 39(1) 59–69.

You have to be a good person to be kind

Kindness isn't only the preserve of saints or monks. You don't have to be perfect to be kind. You just need to be human and every human, even saints (Mother Teresa often spoke of her struggles to be good, or her 'dark night of the soul') are a complex mixture of good and not so good and, in some cases, darn right bad. So, if you feel a bit of a fake doing kind things because you know how often you let your halo slip, perhaps by gossiping or lashing out or being mean, you are no different from everyone else. You are simply being human, and any human can be kind. There is no entry qualification to perform acts of kindness. Just start doing it and see how it makes you feel.

Kindness is easy

Kindness requires great courage. Every time you are kind you are, in fact, stepping outside your comfort zone. Progress only happens *outside* your comfort zone. So, when you get feelings of dread or anxiety, don't always try to run away from them because they are signs that you are stepping outside your comfort zone. You are being called to deal with those feelings and in the process evolve. Laziness and selfishness often take centre stage in your comfort zone, and making the decision to rebel against them and do something that benefits others, sometimes more than yourself, is not for the faint-hearted.

Shouldn't I put myself first?

Of course, you should put yourself first, and that's why the first ways to be kind focus on acts of compassion towards yourself. You can't offer someone a drink from an empty cup. However, as with everything in life, there has to be a balance. If you always put yourself first, even though you may not admit it to yourself, life starts to feel empty. Reaching out to others in kindness is in your DNA, and if you don't activate your kindness genes enough, your emotional, psychological and physical wellbeing will ultimately suffer. The secret is valuing yourself enough to know when your cup is full and you feel secure and strong enough to be kind in a way that does not damage you. Working through the ways to be kind in this book will help you identify when you are at that tipping point.

Kind people finish last

There is a difference between being kind and being weak. Kind people routinely get ignored, taken advantage of or rarely thanked for their efforts, but they are not weak pushovers. In fact, they notice people who are manipulative, rude or lazy and approach them with tact and politeness. They know two wrongs do not make a right. When others aim low, they aim high. They also know how to say 'no' with firmness and grace, and set boundaries when others overstep them. Over time, people gradually begin to recognise them for the responsible and compassionate force for good that they are. Again, the 100 Ways to Be Kind section of this book (Chapters 2–5) will help you to separate weakness from kindness.

It's too late

Perhaps you feel you are set in your ways and it is too late for you to change or take action because you are of a certain age. In some ways, the 'I'm too old' myth is similar to the 'you have to be good to be kind' myth/excuse this section started with. Let's explode it with a true-life example. In 2020, war veteran Tom Moore was about to celebrate his 100th birthday. He decided to do a fundraising event to celebrate his birthday and raise money for health workers at the same time. He set himself a modest fundraising target of £1,000 and promised family and friends online that he would walk laps around his garden with his walker until he achieved it. But little did he know that thousands of people around the world would find out about his efforts. To date, he has raised more than 32 million pounds! More than 125,000 birthday cards were sent to him on his birthday and he has been awarded a knighthood! You are never too old to do something extraordinarily kind.

It really is time to put to rest these limiting messages. I hope this book will clearly show that kindness and gentleness are *not* signs of weakness or despair but of inner strength and resolve. It's also time now to put the last and perhaps most damaging myth to bed.

It won't make any difference

I am sure you have heard the famous story about the little boy who was concerned about the hundreds of starfish washed up on a beach. He started to throw them back in the sea, but a passer-by told him he was wasting his time because beaches all around the world had countless starfish washed up on them and what he was doing would not make any difference. He was fighting a losing battle. But the little boy picked up another starfish and before he threw it back into the sea, he shrugged and said to the passer-by, 'Well, it will make a difference to this one!'

It's easy to get despondent when you are bombarded by negative images daily and there seems so much unkindness and unfairness in the world, but I hope this book will show you that every act of kindness you perform, however small, makes a tremendous difference. The difference starts with you. Helping others makes you feel better – sometimes better than the person you actually help. In some ways, being kind is a very selfish act because you get that well-reported 'helper's high'.[17] But there is nothing wrong with that because, if you feel better, you will treat those you love better. Your act of kindness will not only touch the life of the person you help, but, as research[18] shows, it will make them, in turn, more likely to help someone else. This has been called 'the pay it forward'[19] effect, which is the feeling of gratitude, connection and expansion someone feels when they have received an act of kindness that then inspires them to be kind themselves. In this way, you create a ripple effect of kindness that starts with you and ripples out from person to person.

You really have no idea how much any act of kindness you perform, however small, has the potential to trigger a chain reaction. For example, a kind comment on someone's Facebook post about their missing cat may encourage the person to post a kind comment on the page of someone else who is mourning the death of their pet, and that kind comment may in turn encourage that person to make a donation to an animal shelter. That donation could save the life of an abused puppy. That puppy could be adopted by someone suffering from depression and ultimately save their life. And it all began with your kind comment on a post!

Never underestimate the impact of an act of kindness. Kindness really is contagious.[20] In the words of Amelia Earhart, the pioneering aviator:

---

17 Luks, A. (2001) *The Healing Power of Doing Good*. iUniverse, p.192. Luks coined the term 'helper's high'.

18 Fowler, J. *et al.* (2010) 'Cooperative behaviour cascades in human social networks.' *Proceedings of the National Academy of Sciences*, 107 (12) 5334–5338.

19 This phrase was made popular by Catherine Ryan Hyde's novel of the same phrase, which was later turned into a movie.

20 Barsade, S.G. (2002) 'The ripple effect: Emotional contagion and its influence on group behavior.' *Administrative Science Quarterly*, 47(4) 644–675.

No kind action ever stops with itself. One kind action leads to another. Good example is followed. A single act of kindness throws out roots in all directions, and the roots spring up and make new trees. The greatest work that kindness does to others is that it makes them kind themselves.

How to use this book

The 100 ways to be kind that follow offer you a road map, and your destination is a life of kindness. Many of us may have forgotten how to be kind – it's not something that is taught in schools – and in recent years there hasn't been enough value placed on it. That's changing now due to the radical shift created by the Coronavirus and the racism protests and the long overdue spotlight this has shone on the healing power of kindness, tolerance and compassion to bring much-needed connection, meaning and healing.

You can undertake the 100 ways to be kind in any way that works for you. I recommend going through them in numerical order – performing one (or more) new way to be kind each day for 100 days – because each way to be kind builds on the foundations laid by the previous one. However, if you want to start with one specific section, feel free to do so. The important thing is that you work through all 100 ways to be kind.

> **Be kinder to you:** The first 25 ways to be kind are dedicated to self-compassion or self-care. If you can't be kind to yourself, you are not valuing yourself and simply won't have the energy to offer your kindness to others. Work through these first and give yourself the strongest foundation from which to launch your life of kindness.

> **Be kinder online:** The next 15 ways to be kind focus on your online participation – and for good reason. Like it

or not, we live in an online world and the Coronavirus-enforced isolation highlighted that, more than ever, it can be a lifeline.

Be kinder to others: These 40 ways to be kind highlight the importance of kindness to others: our loved ones, friends, colleagues, strangers, people with different beliefs and backgrounds and even those who are unkind to us, because how we treat others is who we are.

Be kinder to nature: The final 20 ways urge you to be kind to animals, nature and the planet itself.

Each of the chapter titles says 'kinder' rather than kind because, as explained earlier, kindness is already in your DNA. You just need to notice it, value it and activate it, and that's where this book can help you. You will also notice that most of the ways to be kind are focused on simple, everyday actions – practical things you can do rather than setting intentions or doing yoga poses or meditations. Research[21] shows that actions impact our brains as much as thoughts and feelings.

Numerous studies[22] show that your brain is led more by your daily actions than by your thoughts. Change starts with what you repeatedly do – your small everyday actions – regardless of what you are thinking. If you've ever felt your mood boosted after a brisk walk, you will already know the truth of this. I feel there has been too much emphasis in personal development in recent years on thinking, dreaming, affirming, meditating and visualising, and

21 Neal, D. *et al.* (2013) 'How do people adhere to goals when willpower is low? The profits and pitfalls of strong habits.' *American Journal of Personality and Social Psychology*, 104(6) 959–975, doi 10.1037/a0032626.

22 Hobson, N.M. *et al.* (2017) 'Rituals decrease the neural response to performance failure.' *Peer Journal*, e3363, doi: 10.7717/peerj.33633.

not enough on doing. Just as we should judge others by what they do rather than what they say, start holding yourself to the same standard. Life rewards, and others admire, those who walk the talk. Contrary to what you may have been led to believe, you are not what you think, you are what you repeatedly do!

I strongly urge you to carry out at least one way to be kind every day for 100 days. Make it your 100-day compassion challenge. At the outset, don't tell yourself this is forever because that sounds too daunting for your mind to process. Simply tell yourself you will do this for 100 days and then reassess. A hundred days is significant because it is long enough for your daily actions to make a real impact on your brain and help make those kindness 'muscles' so strong that there is no going back because you feel so much happier.

Each day that you incorporate kindness into your life increases your chances of happiness and fulfilment but bear in mind that that clear signs of improvement may not appear for at least four weeks. This is the minimum period of time research[23] suggests it takes for new neural pathways to form in your brain, your kindness 'muscle' to grow stronger, and for there to be a noticeable change in how you think, feel and act.

Some of the 100 ways to be kind will be activities I recommend you repeat daily to get the maximum benefit, but others will be for that day only. Whether you choose to do them daily or not – to risk repeating myself – try to do at least one act of kindness every day, because the aim is to make kindness your way of life rather than something you sometimes do. Your brain responds to repetition, so you need to make being kind what defines you. To do that, you need to take small steps every single day to strengthen those kindness pathways in your brain. (If you

---

23 Lally, P. (2010) 'How are habits formed: Modelling habit formation in the real world.' *European Journal of Social Psychology*, 40(6) 998–1009.

had a hypothetical brain scan the doctors would all nod and say, 'The diagnosis is clear— a very kind person, indeed!') Some of them may feel like small actions, trivial even, but you will find the transformative impact comes from actually doing them and repeating them daily, if appropriate. Your daily actions really can evolve into life-changing results.

Inspiring others

Seeing, reading or hearing about acts of kindness motivates others to be kinder. It alters their responses and behaviour. This is called the third-party or observer effect of kindness, and it's one most of us aren't aware of. I know this for sure, as for many years now I have shared inspiring stories on my social media of acts of kindness my readers have carried out or received, which they have sent to me, and the stories keep pouring in. When you see, read or hear about others being kind – even if you don't know or have never met that person and are watching from a distance or hearing about it online – it makes you feel good about being a human being and you are more likely to be kind or to promote the value of kindness yourself. In this way, kindness really is contagious. Your one act of kindness has the potential to impact hundreds, potentially thousands, more lives without you knowing.

So be kind, do kind things daily, share your stories and notice how they inspire others, setting a train of kindness in motion. (Details about how to connect with me and share your stories, questions and insights can be found at the end of the book. I'd love to hear from you.)

Choose to be kind

How you treat yourself and others, and the world you live in, is who you really are. It does start with you. Yes, the world can feel crazy at times and filled with turmoil and uncertainty. Our first instinct during times of crisis is to try to regain control. We like to think we have control over our lives, but there are always going to be unseen forces over which we will never have control. I'm reminded of that famous Robert Burns' poem 'To a Mouse', in which the mice were busy building their nests, unaware of the plough heading their way. In early 2020, most of the world had absolutely no idea their lives would soon change forever.

Accepting that there are always going to be things that happen in life over which you have no control is an important step for your personal growth. But equally crucial is understanding that there *is* something you do have control over, and that is how you choose to think, feel and act. Nobody but you can make your choices.

You can choose to be kind. And if you choose to be kind, you are not powerless. The choices you make each day from this moment on will define who you are and the world you live in. If you are still unconvinced and feel that the things you do are trivial or don't really matter, here's another commonly used metaphor. Imagine you buy a 1,000-piece puzzle depicting a stunning wildlife scene. You painstakingly complete the puzzle and think it looks so amazing you want to frame it and hang it on your wall. But there is one big problem. One of the pieces is missing. Would you hang that puzzle on the wall with the piece missing? You probably wouldn't, because you know that everyone looking at it would just notice and fixate on the missing piece, rather than admiring the bigger picture.

You are that missing piece.

The world needs you to stand up and be kind – urgently.

CHAPTER 2

25 WAYS TO BE KINDER TO YOURSELF

Three things in human life are important: the first is to be kind; the second is to be kind; and the third is to be kind.
Henry James

Being kind isn't about always putting your own needs and wishes last. It is not an 'others-before-self' mantra or even a 'look after yourself before helping others' guideline. Obviously, if you are suffering from anxiety, poor health or depression, it is essential that you prioritise your own emotional and physical needs – and you can't help others from a position of emotional vulnerability. But in the majority of cases, being kinder to yourself is not about 'shoulds' or 'oughts'. It is much easier and more natural than that. It is just about valuing yourself and carrying that value for yourself with you in everything you think, say and do for yourself and for others.

And you may not have thought about it this way, but your respect for yourself gifts others the opportunity to feel relaxed around you because you are not 'needy', or unconsciously demanding others to 'fix' you. The better care you take of your own needs and the more you value yourself, the easier it is for others to feel boosted rather than drained by your company.

Valuing yourself has the same mood-boosting impact as kindness. It boosts feelings of wellbeing and your expectation of deserving happiness and success. But the chances are that being kind to yourself is something you place as a low priority or feel guilty about doing. If valuing and being kinder to yourself don't come naturally, the following 25 ways to be kind can help you find the path back to the self-esteem that is your birthright.

And, even if you do feel that you value yourself, we all take ourselves for granted or are less than kind to ourselves from time to time. Use the practical suggestions offered here to course-correct and replace any self-doubt or negative criticism with empowering self-compassion.

Bear in mind that, with a few profound exceptions, all the ways to be kinder focus on the transformative and uplifting power of actions – things you can *do* to be kind to yourself. This book is all about bringing the idea of kindness out of your head and into your everyday life, and the best way to do that is to get moving as soon as the day begins. That's why you will notice that the first ten ways to be kind in this section are all designed to be performed first thing. The following ten ways to be kinder to yourself are more suited to daytime, with the remaining five ways to be kinder ideal for evening time. So, if you integrate all 25 ways from waking to sleeping, you'll have a framework for being kinder to yourself for every day and night of your life.

Morning – Way 1: Make your bed

If you want to be kinder to yourself and change your life for the better, making your bed every morning is a powerful and highly effective kick-start. It's also something that you can easily commit to every day. Make a promise to yourself that, from first thing tomorrow, you will make your bed immediately when you get up for the next 100 days. (If you share your bed with someone, you might want to consider making the bed every other day.)

You may think something as trivial as making your bed can't possibly make a difference, but it truly does. How do you feel at the end of your day when, instead of relaxing, you have to sort out your bedding? Not to mention how untidy an unmade bed makes your bedroom look. There is a reason why there is so much emphasis in the military[24] on the importance of making your bed as soon as you get up. It's a powerful sign of self-respect and self-discipline.

In addition, your bedroom is your personal space. It's the place where you can fully relax and unwind. It's a glimpse of who you truly are. It doesn't have to be super tidy, but it does need to be somewhere that makes you feel good about yourself when you spend time in it. If it looks chaotic and uncared for, what message is that sending you about your attitude towards yourself? Your bed is the centrepiece of your bedroom. If your bed is made, it inspires you to ensure that the rest of your bedroom is also a haven of order and tranquillity.

Only you know what makes you feel comfortable and relaxed when it comes to your bedding. But making your bed isn't just about comfort. It's about so much more. Making your own bed gives you a sense of pride, organisation and motivation. It sets the right self-nurturing tone for the day ahead. It also turns your attention first thing to the importance of your everyday actions and how they determine the way you treat yourself and others. The small things really do matter the most. So, what are you waiting for?

Take action

Commit now to making your bed for yourself when you get up in the morning. If you already do this routinely, be sure to transform your bed-making routine into an empowering ritual in which you are fully aware of what you are doing. Don't think about the day

---

24 McRaven, H. (2007) *Make Your Bed.* Michael Joseph.

ahead. Focus all your attention on each action. As you plump your pillows, smooth your sheets and duvet or blankets, remind yourself why accomplishing this first task of the day matters so much for your self-esteem. This is an act of pure kindness towards yourself. When you are finished, spend a few moments admiring your lovingly made masterpiece. Remind yourself that climbing into your bed tonight will bring you feelings of well-deserved comfort and relaxation after a long or busy day.

Morning – Way 2: Find three good things each day

Your second way to be kinder to yourself couldn't be simpler or more obvious. It's spending a few moments each day making a conscious effort to shine a spotlight on three things that you like or appreciate about yourself. There's even scientific backing[25] to prove that focusing on three good things about yourself daily, ideally at the same time so it becomes a ritual, is highly effective in boosting happiness and self-esteem. But for some bizarre reason few of us actually do it. In fact, we do the opposite!

Most of us pay a lot of attention to the harsh critical voice in our head. Perhaps it echoes words you heard during your formative childhood years from carers or teachers but, however it got there, it has taken up residence and is very comfortable living in your head. This exercise encourages you to evict that harsh inner critic and replace it with the kind voice of a loving friend who focuses only on the positive things about you, rather than your vulnerabilities. It will help you become what you should always have been – your own best friend.

Hopefully, from today onwards, thinking about three things that you appreciate about yourself every day will become a quick,

---

25 Siew, T. *et al.* (2017) 'The three good things – the effects of gratitude on wellbeing: a randomised controlled trial.' *Health Psychology*, March 2017 (26) 1.

daily ritual, something you are eager to do because you know how important it is. Just as your brain has kindness 'muscles', it also has gratitude and self-appreciation 'muscles' and the more you flex them by expressing gratitude for yourself, the more your mindset kindly shifts towards positivity.

Take action

All you need to do is set aside a few moments every morning (or every evening if you like, although morning is preferable as it sets the tone for the rest of the day) to list on your phone, computer or notepad three things you like about yourself. It's better to write or type rather than just think them because the action of putting pen to paper or finger to keypad transforms this exercise into something your mind can't ignore. You can put the same three things each day or come up with new ones. They don't have to be earth-shattering. You could simply write that you have a nice smile or that you made your bed this morning. What matters is that you appreciate yourself and don't take the good things about yourself for granted ever again.

This way to be kind is a genuine life-changer if you commit to actually doing it. If you don't think something so obvious can work, you have nothing to lose and everything to gain by simply giving it a try. The important thing is to actually do it, even if you don't feel like it or believe in it. The transformative power is in doing it – and doing it repeatedly.

Morning – Way 3: Be enough

Self-depreciation is an act of extreme unkindness towards yourself. It tends to spring from the erroneous but widely held belief that you are incomplete or not good enough, and the only way to find completeness or a sense of wholeness is outside yourself in other people or things. Self-affirmation is a proven way[26] to counteract this flawed and self-destructive belief.

It's not surprising that many of us feel dissatisfied with who we are. Every day we are bombarded with images of things that are supposed to complete us – from money, to jobs, to relationships, to hairstyles, to 'stuff'. Iconic movies, particularly rom-coms, like *Jerry Maguire*, promote this 'you complete me' myth. And much as I love that spine-tingling song, 'Never Enough' from the movie *The Greatest Showman*, it really is an anthem for an unhappy life in its potent articulation of a burning feeling of incompleteness without success and having more and more. The lead character in *The Greatest Showman* manages to escape from this seductive 'never enough' illusion just in time to save his own chances of happiness. I hope this exercise has the same empowering effect and helps re-programme your mind and body to instinctively accept that the only person who can ever complete you or make you feel whole is *you*. Happiness comes from within.

Take action

Every single day you are going to remind yourself – preferably first thing in the morning when you wake up and your brain-waves are in a suggestible state – that you are and have enough. Remember, your brain doesn't know the difference between opinion or fact, so you are going to have to quite literally change your mind over the coming weeks. You are going to think it, believe it and start doing it.

I don't typically endorse affirmations because I believe in the power of doing rather than thinking, but this is my exception. Affirmations do have the potential to change the way your mind

---

26 Harris, P. *et al.* (2017) 'Self-affirmation improves performance on tasks related to executive functioning.' *Journal of Experimental Social Psychology*, 70, May, 281–285.

is programmed, but the reason many of them don't work is because thinking or saying them isn't enough. You also need to do something to ensure the message gets through to your mind and body, loud and clear.

So, combine your daily affirmation with an action. Before you start your day, grab your phone, open a blank text or email and type the following: 'I am enough and I have enough' and send that message to yourself. Then, during the day whenever you feel that familiar sense of emptiness or that you are not enough or complete without someone or something, find that email or text and read it out loud to yourself at least three times. Hear yourself saying it out loud to remind you of the unique miracle of DNA you are. Let it help you find your sense of completeness from the inside out, rather than the outside in.

Morning – Way 4: Think big

How do you typically get up? I'm guessing you roll out of bed and then shuffle to the bathroom with half-closed eyes lowered to the floor? Today and every day, I'd like you to stop treating yourself in such a small and unkind way. You are going to think and act bigger instead.

If you tend to hunch when you get up, the message you send to your body and brain is that you are small and unimportant. Your body and mind are constantly listening, so don't be surprised if your day mirrors that initial smallness or tone of unimportance back to you. Stretching is a proven stress buster and confidence-booster and there is even some research[27] to suggest that the first overt action you take in the day – typically, getting out of bed – may become the theme for your entire day. Harvard psychologist Amy

---

27 www.businessinsider.com/wake-up-first-thing-morning-amy-cuddy-psychology-2017-7?r=US&IR=T.

Cuddy believes that people who wake up by stretching their bodies in a 'V' shape are more likely to feel confident than those who minimise themselves physically or stay in the foetal position while getting up. Treating yourself to an enormous stretch, perhaps with a battle-cry yawn, when you get out of bed puts you centre stage in your own life – the place you deserve to be.

Stretching big as soon as you get up sounds simple but, like all these ways to be kinder to yourself, it isn't as easy as you think, especially if you have got into the habit of minimising yourself throughout the day by frowning and hunching your shoulders when checking phones or screens. Your mind is led by your actions, so shrinking yourself in this way almost certainly diminishes your thinking and actions and damages your self-esteem.

Take action

Tomorrow when you wake up – and every morning from now on – don't just roll out of bed and hunch the way you have always done. Make a daily ritual out of getting up. Stand up slowly, breathe in deeply and then reach as high as you can on your tiptoes, hands in the air towards the ceiling, and indulge in a mighty stretch. Take as long as you need in this expansive position. Then let your hands fall by your sides, take another deep breath and place them on your waist in a confident superhero pose, with legs apart. Feel big and confident. Make your presence felt. If you can't do your confidence pose in your bedroom, do it in your bathroom or downstairs, but watch your posture as you walk. Stand tall.

Notice how empowering it feels to stretch and become physically bigger than normal. This big morning moment is just for you. It's all about taking special care of yourself and reminding you how important and expansive you are. During the day, if you need to make a decision and find yourself hunching your shoulders and minimising your body, be sure to strike a pose and think and act big again.

Morning – Way 5: Find your happy tune

Over the years, you may find that you listen less and less to music. This exercise is going to ask you to reverse that trend and think younger by making music, in particular upbeat music, a key part of your morning routine. You are going to find your 'happy tune' (or tunes) and in the process feel better about yourself and your life. Letting great music back into every day of your life is one of the kindest and happiest things you can do for yourself.

It isn't entirely clear how, but research[28] definitely indicates that listening to upbeat music can boost your energy, memory and mood significantly. It can also help reduce stress. Listening to music you love or that puts a smile on your face when you wake up and get ready can give you the best possible start and feel-good vibes that potentially last all day. So, if you have unintentionally let music slip out of your life, or not tuned into its self-care potential, it is high time to make music part of your daily life again.

Take action

Nothing could be simpler. Think of upbeat songs or a piece of music that makes you want to tap your feet or get up and dance. Then download it onto your phone or wherever you listen to music. At some point during your morning routine be sure to put your headphones on and listen to your favourite upbeat songs. Listen to the music for at least three to five minutes for the full mood-boosting impact. Make sure the music

---

28 Ferguson, Y. *et al.* (2013) 'Trying to be happier really can work: Two experimental studies.' *The Journal of Positive Psychology*, 8(1) 23–33.

is not played too loud and, if you want to sing or dance along, don't hesitate as singing and dancing can also work wonders. However, if you prefer to listen as you get dressed or brush your teeth, do so. The important thing is that you listen and feel the upbeat energy and joy pulsating through you. Make this your moment of pure joy.

It doesn't really matter which song you choose as long as it is one that makes you feel energised or eager to dance. It is your happy tune. To get you thinking along the right lines here are some tried and tested suggestions for musical kick-starters:

- 'Dancing Queen' by Abba
- 'Don't Stop Me Now' by Queen
- 'Hey Ya!' by OutKast
- 'Heaven Is a Place on Earth' by Belinda Carlisle
- 'Crazy in Love' by Beyoncé
- 'Don't Stop Believin'' by Journey
- 'Happy' by Pharrell Williams

If you prefer classical music that is fine, just make sure it is upbeat and energising, along the lines of Prokofiev's 'Montagues and Capulets'. Losing yourself in music that makes you feel like dancing or marching is one of the best and most enjoyable ways to get your day off to a great start. Just find your happy beat and the rest is easy.

Morning – Way 6: Rise and sparkle

This suggestion may seem contradictory because you probably think a morning lie-in is a treat, but it really isn't – in the long-term it has a draining effect similar to jet lag. Your body clock thrives on a regular waking and sleeping schedule and whenever you mess with that schedule you pay the price with poor concentration and fatigue. In addition, research[29] shows that there is a connection between people who get up early and have success in life. Of course, there are always exceptions, but it seems that early risers are happier and more fulfilled than those who choose to lie in. You see, energy, positivity and discipline are required to rise and sparkle and those are the qualities that increase your chances of success and happiness.

In short, the connection between early rising and success is a proven one so making a commitment to yourself to get up earlier and keep to that earlier waking time is an act of great kindness towards yourself. Successful people just don't lounge around in bed. They get up early to have some peaceful time to themselves, plan their day, tidy up, exercise, meditate, create or simply prepare for the day and, by so doing, give themselves a head start.

Take action

Your instinctive response when you wake up is likely to be to curl into a ball and go back to sleep, so the key is to wake up in the right way and, over time, aim to wake up with the excitement of a child on their birthday, as your body adjusts. Start the night before by putting your alarm clock a distance away from your bed so you have to get up to turn it off. When you wake up, say out loud, 'Wake up now.' This may feel odd, but you are simply taking control of your life by being your own motivational coach. Once up, take a deep breath and switch off your alarm, reminding yourself that getting up earlier is a gift to yourself. Congratulate yourself. And if you struggle to get up when the alarm goes off, try this technique. Say out loud 'five, four, three, two, one' and then get up on one.

---

29 Gulec, M. *et al.* (2013) 'Chronotype effects on general well-being and psychopathology levels in healthy young adults.' *Biological Rhythm Research*, 44(3) 457–468.

You don't have to immediately start waking up at 5 a.m., just begin your day half an hour earlier to start with and then, if you want to wake up even earlier, adjust gradually over time. (Bear in mind that six to eight hours of sleep is considered optimum for most people.) If you feel tired during the day, go to bed earlier, preferably before midnight and, if you work night shifts so have to sleep in the morning, adjust this exercise to suit what would be your 'morning' time. Even if you don't think you are a morning person, just give this way to be kinder to yourself a try for a week or two to see if it makes you feel better.

Morning – Way 7: Forget your phone

What's the first thing you do as soon as you wake up? Chances are it is reach sleepily for your phone to check new messages or what's on your newsfeed. You probably have your phone charging by your bedside overnight, too. Indeed, research[30] has shown that up to 60 per cent of phone users do that so they aren't separated from their phones and can immediately reach for them when they wake up. This way to be kinder to yourself asks you not to use your phone first thing and, better still, not to have your phone charging in your bedroom either. Instead, you need to do something else and put the focus firmly on *you*.

Mobile phone addiction[31] is a growing cause for concern, with some studies[32] showing we are checking our phones up to a staggering 150 times a day, which is not good for our mental, emotional and physical wellbeing. I'm not advising against phone

---

30 www.dailymail.co.uk/health/article-2577824/Why-NEVER-mobile-bedroom.html.

31 Li, L. (2019) 'Over-connected? A qualitative exploration of smartphone addiction among working adults in China.' BMC Psychiatry, 19, 186.

32 www.inc.com/john-brandon/science-says-this-is-the-reason-millennials-check-their-phones-150-times-per-day.html.

use here, just saying that you need to downgrade the importance of your phone. And the best way to do that is to avoid sleeping and waking up with it!

If the first thing you do every morning is check your phone, the tone you are setting for the day is that the messages, memes and newsfeeds on your phone are more important to you than your own wellbeing. Those early waking moments are sacred. They set the tone for your day ahead. So, you need to make your own thoughts, feelings and dreams the absolute priority in those precious early moments. You are not being selfish here, you are being respectful and kind to yourself and, ultimately, kinder to others because by focusing on yourself first thing, you boost your own energy and your ability to give effectively to others.

Take action

The night before, make sure you put your phone on charge in a room other than your bedroom and avoid using it as an alarm clock. If you are worried you could miss an urgent message overnight, tell your loved ones you are offline and, for anything super-urgent, simply to call you. You may wish to get yourself a good old-fashioned alarm clock, perhaps even with clock hands rather than a digital display.

The next morning when you wake up, resist rushing to check your phone for at least half an hour. Use those first precious minutes of the day to reflect, gather your thoughts, stretch, tidy up, eat a healthy breakfast, make your bed, plan your day ahead and take care of yourself. If the first half an hour or so of your day isn't yours, the chances are the rest of your day won't be either. So, if you want to take the very best care of yourself and change your life for the better, don't reach for your phone first thing – tune into yourself instead.

Morning – Way 8: Drink it in

What's the first drink you have in the morning? Is it orange, lemon or apple juice? A coffee? A tea or herbal brew? Or do you reach for a sugary soda for an immediate energy boost?

Did you know that the optimum drink first thing, the drink that is kindest to your body and mind, isn't any of these traditional breakfast favourites? It is a humble glass of room-temperature water. Most of us truly underestimate just how important water is for our wellbeing, but as this way to be kinder to yourself makes clear – water is your life!

Drinking water when you get up (before drinking or eating anything else) makes perfect sense when you consider your body consists of up to 60 per cent water. You can't live without water because every cell and tissue in your body needs it to function. You can live without food far longer than you can live without water. Research has also shown that drinking enough water during the day is crucial for concentration and brain function[33] (up to 85 per cent of the brain is made up of water) and it helps you detoxify and digest food better, so it's great for weight management. And, like kindness, it can make you look younger because it improves circulation and blood flow and makes your skin glow. It is no exaggeration to say that nourishing, cleansing, refreshing, healing water is the elixir of life. It helps you think clearly, feel good and look better. There really is nothing kinder you can do for your holistic wellbeing than to drink a glass of water first thing.

Take action

Before you get dressed, eat breakfast or drink anything else, sip a glass of water slowly. Make sure your water is at room tempera-

---

33 www.cambridge.org/core/journals/british-journal-of-nutrition/article/mild-dehydrationimpairscognitive-performance-and-mood-of-men/3388AB36B8 DF73E844C9AD19271A75BF.

ture rather than ice cold, as this is easier for digestion. As you drink, think about how you are replenishing your fluid intake and how essential water is for all life.

Be sure to sit down, too, as you drink. You typically sit down to eat for digestive reasons, so pay the same mindful attention to drinking your water. Between each sip of water, be mindful of the refreshment you are giving your mind and body. Take a small sip, swallow and then breathe. Repeat until you completely empty your glass. And continue this newfound respect for water throughout the day. Be aware that if you feel thirsty you are already dehydrated, so make sure you drink enough and carry water with you when you go out if you know you won't have access to any. If your urine is dark yellow and your lips and eyes feel dry, you urgently need to drink more water. Around eight glasses a day are recommended by health experts, but everyone is different. If you drink a glass of water first thing, sip more throughout the day and notice and respond to any thirst cues, you will be drinking the right amount for you.

Morning – Way 9: Breathe deeply

Close your eyes and take a deep breath. Don't breathe in from your chest, inhale deeply from your belly until you can breathe in no more and then exhale loudly. Feels great, doesn't it? So why not be kinder to yourself by incorporating a few minutes of deep breathing into your morning routine?

Countless studies[34] have proven that breathing deeply and slowly can boost energy, ease stress and make you feel better. It may also improve immunity. The chances are that, as you go about your busy day, you have got into the habit of breathing shallowly.

---

34 Zaccaro, A. *et al.* (2018) 'How breath-control can change your life: A systematic review on psycho-physiological correlates of slow breathing.' *Frontiers in Human Neuroscience*, 12: 353.

But the health benefits of deep breathing are incredible – healers specialise in it and books have been written about it. However, despite this, the message still isn't getting through loud and clear. The reason is probably because it seems too simple and easy, almost too good to be true. But the benefits of deep breathing are so remarkable that anyone who wants to change their life for the better would be foolish not to set aside a few moments each day to take a look at the way they are breathing and adjust accordingly.

Take action

Each morning, as you are getting ready to start your day, set aside a few minutes to focus on your breathing. First, notice how you breathe normally. If you can't hear yourself breathing or see any movement in your chest, you are breathing shallowly. Obviously, you can't breathe deeply all the time – and go around huffing and puffing during the day – so that's why doing some slow, deep-breathing exercises first thing can really be beneficial.

For deep breathing to be effective you need to breathe in and out slowly and deeply from your stomach (abdomen) and not your lungs (chest). It is also important to breathe in through your nose and out through your mouth. So, stand or sit tall, place your hand on your stomach and feel it expand as you breathe in slowly through your nose, feeling your lungs fill up completely. Then, with your lungs full, hold for a second or two and then exhale completely, pushing all the air out of your lungs as you do so. It's fine to hold your nose closed and even make a noise when you exhale.

Breathing from your stomach may feel strange or odd at first, but it is the way babies breathe and it won't take you long to start feeling more natural. I recommend doing five inhales and five exhales and then building up to ten each morning. As you do this exercise, remind yourself that this is not just about breathing better, it is about doing something good for yourself. Breathing is something you have to do anyway – so you may as well start doing it well and in a way that is kind to yourself.

Morning – Way 10: Yawn and smile

Complete your morning routine with a big yawn and a huge smile at yourself in the mirror. Both yawning and smiling can make you feel better. Yawning stretches your jaw muscles and increases blood flow to your neck, face and head. The sharp intake of air also helps calm and cool your brain. And smiling can really boost your mood – research[35] consistently shows that it can ease stress and boost energy. There was a fascinating yearbook profile[36] done by Wayne State University in Detroit, which showed that those who had the biggest smiles lived the longest. If you don't feel like yawning or smiling, do it anyway because studies demonstrate that activating your mouth and eye muscles can trick your brain into thinking you are happy. Remember, your brain is led by your actions.

It's important to do this exercise in the morning in front of a mirror because meeting the most important person in your life – you – with a massive grin, even if feels unnatural, reminds you that your relationship with yourself sets the tone for your relationship with everyone else. Sure, the scientist Duchenne[37] proved it's easy for others to tell the difference between real and fake smiles, but your brain can't. It just responds to your facial muscle movement, so the more you practise, the easier and more natural smiling will become.

---

35 Kraft, T. *et al.* (2012) 'Grin and bear it: The influence of manipulated facial expression on the stress response.' *Psychological Science*, 23(11) 1372–1378.
36 Abel, E. *et al.* (2010) 'Smile intensity in photographs predicts longevity.' *Psychological Science*, 21(4) 542–544.
37 Duchenne G.B. (1990) The mechanism of human facial expression, trans. R.A. Cuthbertson, Cambridge University Press.

Take action

Before you start your day, be sure to find a moment to stand in front of the mirror. First, close your eyes and enjoy a big yawn. Then, open them, look into them in the mirror and greet yourself with a massive smile. Be sure to involve both corners of your mouth and your eye sockets. It can help to recall a time when you felt really happy or to imagine someone giving you a surprise bunch of flowers or (my personal favourite) handing you a puppy to hold.

As you smile, remind yourself that smiling more makes you look and feel good and may also help you live a longer, healthier and happier life. Convince your brain you feel great and then, as you go about your day, smile as often as you can. Smile with your teeth until your heart joins in, and notice how differently others respond to you. Like yawning, smiling is contagious and if you smile and look positive, others are far more likely to smile and be kind to you in return. Even if you are working online, talking on the phone or typing messages, try smiling more. Others sense when someone is smiling even if they can't actually see their face.

It's really very simple: kind people smile more at themselves and others.

Daytime – Way 11: Listen to yourself

If someone you were close to confided in you that they felt terrible, your instinctive reaction would not be negative or critical or to tell them it serves them right. You just wouldn't speak to someone you cared about so coldly, would you?

Then why do we typically treat ourselves so harshly? Research[38] clearly shows that people who are compassionate towards them-

---

38 Neff, K.D. (2011) 'Self-compassion, self-esteem, and well-being.' *Social and Personality Psychology Compass*, 5(1) 1–12.

selves feel happier, healthier and more fulfilled. 'Self-love' is a big term and it's one that many of us feel uncomfortable with, perhaps because we associate it with being selfish or arrogant. But self-love is not narcissism, it is simply being compassionate or kind to yourself whenever you feel low or when you've made a mistake. It is acknowledging that it really is okay to feel down at times and that all humans make mistakes and experience grief, self-doubt and suffering. It is speaking kindly to yourself.

Take action

Today, and every time you feel your mood dipping or your harsh inner critic pulling you down, try this proven exercise to help boost your mood and self-esteem.

Grab your phone and open up a blank email or text. Address that email or text to yourself. Then, in the subject heading, write 'Listen to me' or something similar. Start the message with your name and then in the second person write down how you are feeling, what you feel is going wrong and what you want or hope to happen. For example, type 'Dear Theresa, I know you wanted your latest post on social media to help people and are disappointed that it didn't get the response you hoped for' or 'Dear Theresa, I know you regret saying or doing what you did, and this wasn't your intention but...' Then type a line or so to suggest empathy and compassion for what you are going through, so you can see your feelings are ones that all humans have at some point, such as, 'it's impossible to be perfect' or 'everyone makes mistakes'.

Conclude your message to yourself by offering kind words of encouragement or, if you can't think of any advice, simply find a phrase that resonates, like 'time heals' or 'you'll get through this' or 'I believe in you'. Step outside yourself and imagine what you would say to someone you loved who was feeling the way you do. Then, send the email to yourself and read it out loud.

This exercise may feel odd at first, but its power is in the repetition. Studies[39] have shown that writing a self-compassionate letter to yourself for at least seven days in a row in the second person will make you feel better. Give it a try. Keep doing it until it feels natural. You have nothing to lose but self-doubt.

Daytime – Way 12: Laugh out loud

Making sure you smile or laugh during your day is one of the simplest and most effective ways to boost your energy and mood, release tension and take the best care of yourself.

There is plenty of research[40] to suggest that laughing is not just welcome news for your mental and emotional health but also for your physical wellbeing. It seems that laughter can decrease blood pressure, stimulate circulation, increase antibodies that boost immunity and lower cortisol, the stress hormone. Laughter also enhances your intake of oxygen-rich air, stimulates the heart, lungs and muscles, and increases the feel-good endorphins that are released by your brain. There really is no downside to laughing and the more you laugh during the day, the better.

Of course, there are sombre days, and occasions and times when laughter is not appropriate or respectful. But there are far more times when a much-needed injection of humour can be transformative. Humour can bring humanity and heart to even the most solemn of occasions. I was at a funeral recently and, alongside the tears, there was a lot of laughter as those attending knew the deceased wanted everyone to remember him with a smile. And that's profound life wisdom – there's nothing more satisfying than injecting laughter into every day.

---

39 Shapira, L.B. & Mongrain, M. (2010) 'The benefits of self-compassion and optimism exercises for individuals vulnerable to depression.' *Journal of Positive Psychology*, 5, 377–389.

40 www.ncbi.nlm.nih.gov/pmc/articles/PMC2814549.

Take action

If you feel you aren't a naturally funny person, don't worry. You may not believe it, but humour is something that can be learned. You just need to practise every day.

Some time today and every day, set aside at least five minutes to watch, read or think about something that makes you laugh, not silently but out loud. Use your phone to do an online search for funny clips on YouTube or memes filled with good-natured humour, or watch your favourite comedian doing stand-up, or read a funny book or cartoon. Alternatively, seek out jokes or anecdotes you can memorise and perhaps use when it is appropriate to bring laughter into a situation. Do bear in mind that some forms of humour aren't appropriate and use your judgement to discern a great joke from a hurtful one.

Don't forget that it is those closest to us – loved ones, family and friends – that often have the power to make us smile the most. During the lockdown, FaceTime chats with the people I cared about were the times I laughed the most I've done in years, so even if you can't catch up with people in person you can still connect online to make each other laugh. We pick up the phone to speak to loved ones not just to see how they are and catch up on their news but also because we need them to help us see the lighter side of life.

There are so many ways to smile for you to discover, but if you can't find anything that makes you laugh naturally, try laughing out loud for two minutes or until you are out of breath. This is going to feel odd and very forced at first, but give it a try. Just fake it and exercise those laughing 'muscles' because your brain and body can't tell the difference. Smile first, break out into a chuckle, then laugh. Notice how you feel afterwards. Do you feel more relaxed? That's the wonder of laughter at work.

Children laugh so naturally, but over time they laugh less and less. As a child, laughter probably came naturally to you, but as adults we become so serious. Let your newfound knowledge of the myriad of health and mood-elevating benefits of laughter encourage you to seek out the lighter side of life.

Daytime – Way 13: Praise yourself

Over the years, I've lost count of the correspondence people have sent me saying how worried they are about what other people think. The advent of social media has made this ever more prevalent, because every time we post or update, we see in real time how many people 'like' and comment on our contributions – and getting no reaction can feel like such a rejection. So why put yourself through this?

Handing over your self-worth to the whims and judgements of others is an act of extreme unkindness towards yourself. From now on you are going to stop looking for praise and validation from others and praise yourself instead. Research[41] has shown that a positive self-view, affirming your value as an individual and focusing on aspects of your personality you are proud of, can activate areas of the brain associated with feelings of confidence and self-worth. Although positive actions matter the most, the kinder your thoughts and words are about yourself, the easier it is to do kind things for yourself. So today and every day, you are going to place your opinion of yourself above others' opinions of you.

Stop waiting for outside validation and validate yourself instead. If something feels right or good, it doesn't matter what other people think or say. Praise yourself whenever you do a good job or when you do something you feel deserves praise. This isn't to say you should never listen to advice or constructive criticism

---

41 Cascio, C. *et al.* (2016) 'Self-affirmation activates brain systems associated with self-related processing and reward and is reinforced by future orientation.' *Social, Cognitive and Affective Neuroscience*, 11(4) 621–629.

from others – of course you should, as this is one of the best ways to improve, learn and grow. The secret is not to personalise it.

After all, there's only one person in your life you are always going to be in a close relationship with and that person is you. So, you may as well be as kind to yourself as possible.

Take action

Every time you do something you are proud of or feel deserves credit, make a point of pausing for a few moments and saying, 'Well done… (add your name here)' out loud or silently. Give yourself the credit. Tell yourself how good you feel or how proud you are of yourself.

Before you go to bed, review all those moments in your day when you did something well. Pat yourself on the back and relish your achievements. Maybe you settled for an apple instead of a bar of chocolate, or finished a task that needed completing, or you finally tidied up your sock drawer. Whatever it was, reward yourself by doing something you love. It could be relaxing in a warm bath, watching your favourite movie or losing yourself in a good book. It doesn't matter what it is, just make a point of rewarding yourself for things you believe you have done well.

Remember, your own opinion of yourself is the only one that matters!

Daytime – Way 14: Fidget around

Ignore all those people who told you when you were a child to stop fidgeting, because fidgeting is good for you, according to research.[42] It has been shown to boost memory, lower stress and

---

42 Johnson, G. *et al.* (2016) 'Sitting time, fidgeting, and all-cause mortality in the UK women's cohort study.' *American Journal of Preventative Medicine*, 50(2) 154–160.

ease boredom because, fidgeting, such as drumming your fingers or tapping your pen, gives your brain something to focus on. If you are like most people these days, you probably spend a lot of your day sitting down, perhaps driving or working at a desk, and this sedentary lifestyle isn't good for you. Human beings were born to be human 'doings' – constantly on the move in search of food. So, the best, simplest and kindest to yourself solution is to move more, but if you can't find time to exercise, then fidget.

You already know exercise is good for your health and wellbeing. Study after study[43] proves it to be an essential ingredient for a healthier, happier and longer life. It's easy to make excuses to avoid regular exercise, but if you are serious about being kinder towards yourself, a minimum of 20 minutes' daily exercise is nonnegotiable. There is no right or wrong exercise and it doesn't have to be anything complicated – a brisk walk will do. Just decide what type you enjoy doing, whether that be walking, running, cycling, swimming, dancing or sport, and make sure you do it every day, without fail. If you can exercise outdoors in natural daylight that's ideal, because a lack of natural daylight can impact your mood, and your ability to concentrate and sleep well at night. But don't stop there. This way to be kinder to yourself encourages you to be more active throughout the day, and not just think of exercise as a separate thing. And the simplest and easiest way to incorporate more movement into your life is to become a fidget.

Take action

Treat your daily exercise as the sacred act of kindness towards yourself that it is but extend that kindness to the entire day. Whenever

43 Robinson, M.M. *et al.* (2017) 'Enhanced protein translation underlies improved metabolic and physical adaptations to different exercise training modes in young and old humans.' *Cell Metabolism*, 25(3) 581; https://psychcentral.com/blog/10-health-benefits-of-daily-exercise.

you are required to sit for long periods of time, tap your toes, shake your legs and keep your body in motion. Drumming your fingers can also help you concentrate. Think of those tennis players who bounce the ball before hitting a massive serve. The ball bouncing has no real purpose except as a ritual to increase their focus.

Be discreet about your fidgeting, but if anyone notices, tell them fidgeting is good for you. And if your day involves lots of standing, be sure to fidget with your posture too. The ideal standing or sitting posture is one that constantly changes every ten or so minutes, so keep shifting your body. And when you fidget, feel grateful that something so natural and simple is a health- and concentration-boosting gift you can give to yourself anytime, anywhere.

Daytime – Way 15: Challenge your brain

Your body loves routine. For example, it thrives when you get up and go to bed at the same time or when you exercise regularly and eat healthy meals at roughly the same time each day. Your brain, however, has very different needs. It doesn't want routine, it wants variety – it's constantly hungry for change because, as research[44] has shown, new experiences form new neural pathways and can quite literally grow your brainpower. Therefore, the kindest thing you can do for your insatiable brain is to constantly feed it new experiences. The chances are your day involves some fairly predictable routines. Your brain knows those routines well and helps you carry them out on autopilot, with as little energy and focus as possible. Predictable routines offer your brain very little opportunity to form new neural pathways with new experiences. So, to keep your brain nimble, you need to surprise it constantly.

---

44 Alvarez, D.D. *et al.* (2016) 'A disynaptic feedback network activated by experience promotes the integration of new granule cells.' *Science*, 354, 459–465.

Take action

Do something familiar in a different way today and every day. This can be sitting at a different seat in your living room for a different perspective or shopping online at a different store. It doesn't matter how long it takes you to learn how to do something new, just remind yourself that getting out of your comfort zone, doing the unexpected, learning and experiencing new things all expand your brain.

The possibilities to surprise and occupy your novelty-hungry brain every single day are infinite. Don't fall into the trap of thinking you are too old to do things a different way or learn something new – you can continue to expand your brainpower at any age. Indeed, the more active[45] you keep your brain as you age, the less likely it is that you will suffer from age-related memory loss and cognitive decline.

If you are stuck for ideas, here are some to get you started. You'll see that most of them are very small changes, but they can make a world of difference to your brain:

- Brush your teeth using your non-dominant hand.
- Learn a new word every day and make a point of using it in conversation.
- Listen to music you wouldn't normally listen to.
- Read a book about a subject you know nothing about.
- Skip instead of walking.
- Learn a new language or skill, even if it's something simple like folding a napkin correctly.
- Take a different route to work or to the shops.
- Play some number games or do crosswords instead of watching a screen.

45 Antoniou, M. *et al.* (2013) 'Foreign language training as cognitive therapy for age-related cognitive decline: A hypothesis for future research.' *Neuroscience & Biobehavioral Reviews*, 37(10,2) 2689–2698.

Whatever it is, just make sure you notice mindfully how good doing something completely different from what you normally do makes you and your brain feel.

Daytime – Way 16: Reflection time

Encouragement to look and feel good seems to be everywhere these days. It's not surprising that narcissistic personality traits are on the increase and that selfies abound. In times past, people took pictures of the places they visited, but now we all put ourselves centre stage – what we are doing, who we are meeting or where we are is secondary. It's all about how we look in a setting.

All this focus on looking good can tilt the balance away from self-esteem towards self-deception and vanity. It can also encourage you to compare yourself to others, be unrealistic about your abilities and believe the way you look and what you own are more significant than the person you are and what you do. And, when things don't work out or you have a 'bad hair day', you can feel like a complete failure. This emphasis on looking good can cause anxiety and depression. That's why this way to be kinder to yourself urges you to lovingly accept and forgive yourself every time you don't feel or look great.

If you are like most people, you are probably not flexing your self-compassion 'muscle' as much as you should so this way to be kind gives it a much-needed workout. The exercise is a meditation of sorts because meditation has been scientifically proven[46] to boost compassionate behaviour towards yourself and others. The more you do this exercise, the more likely it is that when you don't feel or look great, self-compassion rather than disappointment becomes your default position.

---

46 Graser, J. *et al.* (2018) 'Compassion and loving-kindness meditation: An overview and prospects for the application in clinical samples.' *Harvard Review of Psychiatry*, 26(4) 201–215.

Take action

You need ten minutes for this meditation and ideally somewhere you can be alone and undisturbed. Be warned that the first time you do it, you may feel overwhelmed or emotional as it's incredibly powerful. If emotions do bubble to the surface, don't repress or stifle them, simply allow them to flow.

Stand or sit in front of a mirror and take a look at your face in detail. Stare at your face in silence for five minutes. Notice any thoughts from your inner critic that come into your mind. Don't interact with them, just notice them and let them go. Don't try to alter, think, say or do anything. Then, take a deep breath, close your eyes for a few moments and open them again. This time, look deep into your own eyes and send loving compassion and forgiveness to your reflection for five minutes.

Noticing yourself, mindfully and in a detached way, from the point of view of your inner critic and then from the viewpoint of someone sending unconditional acceptance and healing is incredibly revealing. You will meet the authentic you and, when this happens, you can do the most empowering and kindest thing of all for yourself – send yourself unconditional forgiveness, compassion and love.

Daytime – Way 17: Comfort your body

Good physical health is the foundation stone of a fulfilling and happy life, but it is often overlooked because we tend to take our health for granted until we lose it. If you truly want to be kinder to yourself, it is absolutely essential that you make protecting and nurturing your body a daily priority. So, this way to be kind focuses on being kinder to your body to remind you that self-compassion needs to be holistic and a natural part of your day.

Take action

Every day, make a promise to yourself that you will give yourself a shot of self-compassion by taking the very best care of your physical health that you can. Eat healthily. Exercise regularly. Take a brisk walk outside in the fresh air. Establish a regular sleeping and waking schedule and, if you feel tired, take a break and lie down.

You can also treat yourself by doing your own daily hand massage.[47] As you perform it, think about how hard your hands work for you every day, especially if you spend a lot of time typing or hand-washing. Your hands need pampering. You can do this exercise with or without moisturising cream, but it tends to feel easier with moisturiser.

Start your massage concentrating on one hand first. Pinch the tip of each finger and thumb gently with the fingers of your other hand. Then massage each finger in turn from knuckle to tip before slowly pulling outward on each finger in the same direction. Firmly massage the skin in between each finger and massage the back of your hand, with your thumb working in-between the knuckles. Then turn your hand over and massage your inner wrist and the palm of your hand with the thumb and knuckles of your other hand. Repeat the entire process with your other hand.

If you enjoy this self-soothing treat, you may want to treat yourself to a head massage,[48] which has been shown to ease stress, improve circulation, relieve tension and improve mood.

---

47 Mobini, M. *et al.* (2017) 'The effect of hand reflexology on anxiety in patients undergoing coronary angiography: A single-blind randomised controlled trial.' *Complementary Therapies in Clinical Practice*, 27, 31–36.

48 Howard, V. *et al.* (2013) 'Using Indian head massage to aid recovery.' *Nursing Times*, 109(25) 14–16.
    Begin by placing your thumbs on your temples and let the fingers of both hands rest on your forehead. Apply pressure and then release that pressure in a circular massaging movement. Keeping your fingers and thumbs in position slide your hands up your forehead towards your hairline keeping the circular movement going. Once you reach the top of your head apply

Daytime – Way 18: Lighten your load

You may not realise it, but the untidier your living and working areas are, the harder it is for you to think clearly. A chaotic disorganised work or study environment stresses out your brain and leads to poor concentration and foggy thinking. Clutter is a symbol of disorganisation and confusion, and research[49] has shown that stress hormones are released when you are surrounded by disorder. In short, mess equals stress and has a massive psychological impact on you.

A little order can help you think more clearly, as well as benefit your concentration and creativity, so bringing some organisation into your life is a simple but highly effective way to be kinder to your mind. The more organised you are, the calmer and more in control you feel and the better you are able to concentrate, focus and remember. This isn't to say you need to be super-organised, you just need to make sure there is a certain method to your madness. Your mind will thank you for it.

Take action

This way to be kinder to yourself encourages you to make sure that you tidy at least one thing today in your home or work environment. It doesn't have to be anything dramatic or a big undertaking, such as a spring clean. It can be as simple as organising your store cupboard, sorting out the items in your coat pockets, deleting items on your computer desktop that you don't use any more or unsubscribing from junk mail on your phone.

---

firm pressure to the top of your head and then release. Move down the back of your scalp and continue the circular pressure and release process as before with your thumbs and fingers. Once you reach the base of your skull, repeat the process from the back to the front of your head.

49 http://magazine.ucla.edu/features/the-clutter-culture.

There is always something that needs organising a little better in your life. Give what you don't need to charity and throw away anything that is broken or can't be recycled. Declutter and organise what is left into piles, files or categories, so you can easily find them if you need them or navigate from them to where you need to go. Set up a pending or 'to-do' pile of papers or digital files that are urgent, give yourself deadlines and create reminders for those deadlines. If you keep losing your keys, phone or wallet, set aside a bowl or a special place to keep them, and remind yourself always to put them there so you can find them quickly and easily.

Just a few moments of tidying can have immediate results when you are feeling overwhelmed or stressed. One of the biggest reasons many of us avoid decluttering is because we can't face it, but if you start small, with one drawer, one cupboard or one bag at a time, harmony and order gradually become a stronger theme in your life. Simply commit to one act of tidying up and decluttering every day – it can be as big or as small as you like. Your mind will thank you for it and reward you with better concentration and creativity. As you tidy up, consciously remind yourself that you are clearing out negative energy and being kind to yourself by lightening your mental load.

Daytime – Way 19: Take your heart

Your heart is more than just an organ in your body, it is where your feelings originate, and it has a power and a wisdom all of its own. Studies from the HeartMath Institute[50] show that when you experience feelings of love towards yourself and others, your heart beats in a calmer and gentler way, whereas stress and fear have the opposite effect. They have a negative impact on your heart rate and health. And when you are being kind and loving,

---

50 www.heartmath.org.

your heart is in a transcendent state that researchers[51] call 'heart coherence', which means your heart, mind and body are in perfect harmony.

The problem is that many of us simply don't take the time to tune into the love, wisdom and power of our hearts. We are too busy and there are too many distractions preventing us from listening to its gentle messages. This way to be kind is all about helping you to reconnect with the intuitive power and wisdom of your mighty heart.

Take action

At some point in your day, take a few peaceful moments to yourself in a place where you won't be disturbed. Then, gently place your left hand on your heart. After a while you will feel and perhaps even hear it beating. Tune into that heartbeat and breathe deeply. Inhale and exhale with your beating heart as your guide. Then, when you feel ready, close your eyes and connect to the rhythm of your heart. Hear what it is trying to tell you.

At first you may hear nothing but the sound of your beating heart, and that is fine because there is power in this heart reconnection. But if you do this exercise every day, in time you will start to hear your heart speaking to you, not in words or thoughts but through a heartfelt feeling about what is best and right for you. Indeed, there is research[52] to show that the first place your intuition talks to you may well be through the beating of your heart. The more you connect to your heart rate on a daily basis, the more intuitive and heart-centred you become every day.

Every time you need to make a decision, do this exercise to help you check in with your heart's messages and hear its wisdom. It's

---

51 de Page, B. (2014) *The Power of the Heart: Finding your True Purpose in Life.* Schuster.

52 www.deanradin.com/evidence/Mossbridge2012Presentiment.pdf.

truly worth the effort as your heart is the best friend and mentor you can ever have. It knows what is best for you before even you do.

To ensure you never leave your heart out of any decision-making process again, you may want to put a daily alert on your phone with a heart emoji. Then, when the alert goes off, let it remind you always to take care of the needs of your heart and to consider the wisdom in its messages as you go about your daily life.

Daytime – Way 20: The setting sun

It's not always easy to be kind to yourself. Everyday life can be full of stress and distraction and it can sometimes be hard to get a sense of perspective, especially if you are feeling overwhelmed or negative. But there is something very kind and natural you can do towards the end of each day to give yourself a comforting and reassuring sense of perspective when you need it the most. Simply gaze in awe at the wonder of a sunset.

Research[53] shows that gazing at the sun setting can significantly ease stress and boost your mood and help you find much-needed inner peace. It can also make you feel kinder and more compassionate towards yourself and others because it fills you with a sense of awe and wonder and reminds you that you are part of something infinitely bigger and greater than yourself. It can be a deeply transformative and healing experience, whether you are spiritual or not, as there are cognitive benefits to simply letting your mind wander in any direction it wishes to go, according to some brain-scan studies[54] which show that the default network of the brain is involved in mind-wandering and this is linked to greater creativity. It seems that when the mind is idle, the areas

53 Piff, l.K. *et al.* (2015) 'Awe, the small self, and prosocial behavior.' *Journal of Personality and Social Psychology*, 108(6) 883; Zhang, J. *et al.*

54 https://greatergood.berkeley.edu/article/item/how_mind_wandering_may_be_good_for_you.

in the brain that can solve problems creatively are automatically triggered. So, who knows what dreams this exercise can ignite within you!

Take action

Earlier in the day, find out when the sun is going to be setting and set a timer to remind you to check it out. When the timer goes off, if weather permits, be sure to go outside and find a comfortable and safe place to stand or sit down to watch the unfolding magic. Relax and gaze indirectly (looking directly at the sun isn't good for your eyes) at the melting tapestry of natural beauty. As you gaze, let all your stresses and anxieties fade away with the setting sun.

If it's not possible to go outside you can do this exercise near a window with a good view of the setting sun or perhaps you could use a sunset clock. However you focus your attention on the setting sun, allow the experience to fill you with feelings of deeper inner calm and peace. Let your mind wander as you watch, since the benefits of a wandering mind are at their greatest when you are unaware it is wandering. Focus your attention on observing the setting scene, rather than on any issues or problems you may have.

You may want to take a photograph when you feel the sky is at its most beautiful, and don't be surprised if you feel a tingle of excitement when you take the photo. This is because you are connecting emotionally to the Earth and being reminded, in the words of 'Desiderata', that you are a creation of the universe, no less than the clouds and the stars. You have a right to be here. You are part of something infinite and miraculous. You are amazing and you are loved.

Note: This act of self-kindness lays the foundations and prepares the path ahead for ways 81–100, being kinder to nature.

Evening – Way 21: Look back at your choices

As your day draws to a close, it's time for some reflection on the choices you made during the day. Were they in your best interests?

If you believe in karma, every action has a reaction or generates an energy that returns to you in some way. If you choose actions that are kind to yourself, the healing energy will multiply either through positive things happening to you or through you gaining a sense of deep inner peace. But whether or not you believe in karma, reflecting on your actions every evening is an empowering thing to do because it makes you conscious or aware of the choices you make daily and the role you play in shaping the narrative of your life.

Reflecting on your actions and the consequences of them can also help you cope better with the reactions, opinions and actions of other people. One personal growth theme that features time and again in self-help literature[55] is that whatever other people say or do is not about you but about them. If someone unjustly hurts or upsets you, this is really how they feel about themselves because hurt people hurt others. Rise above it.

Take action

Look back on your day from the moment you got up and ask yourself what the consequences of each choice you made for yourself were. For example, if you chose not to exercise, how does that make you feel now? Research[56] shows that tuning into our feelings when we think about our life choices can help us make better decisions. If you don't like how a certain choice makes you feel when you reflect on it, make a conscious decision to be

---

55 Ruiz, D.M. (1997) *The Four Agreements*. Amber-Allen Publishing.

56 www.medicaldaily.com/science-decision-making-5-surprising-ways-we-make-life-choices-337546.

kinder to yourself the following day, so you can feel good about yourself and your life tomorrow – and every evening.

Reflecting on your life choices can also help you re-programme your natural reaction when others upset you. Instead of allowing them to dictate how you feel, you don't have to give them your power. If their opinion or action was constructive, learn from it but, if not, let it go, accept that not everyone will 'get' you and don't take anything people say or do personally. It's about them, not you.

Focus your attention on what you can control in your life. You can't control other people's reactions, opinions and actions, but you can control your own life choices and the things you do every day. A fulfilling life is one that is built from the small but important choices you make every single day. If there were things you did during the day that make you feel diminished or disappointed, write down a to-do list for tomorrow and ensure that tomorrow is a day when you can rest your head on the pillow feeling content because you had a good day and did the kindest possible things for yourself.

Note: This act of self-kindness lays the foundation and prepares the path ahead for ways 41–80, being kinder to others.

Evening – Way 22: Become a bookworm

The chances are that when you have finished your day or have some free time in the evening your preferred way to relax is to scroll through your social media and newsfeeds on your phone or watch TV box sets, movies or other videos online. There is nothing wrong with this – indeed it can be wonderfully informative, entertaining and relaxing – but today's way to be kinder to yourself is going to encourage you to make reading a good book your first choice whenever you have some free time and want to do something really kind for yourself.

Reading is not just enriching and entertaining, it has many benefits[57] for your wellbeing, according to research. It can boost your vocabulary and memory as well as your concentration and creativity by enhancing connectivity in the brain. It's also a great way to ease stress and learn new things. Knowledge is power and well-read people are often better equipped to deal with life's challenges. Last, but by no means least, reading is fun. However intelligent and well-made TV and video productions might be, they can't beat the brain-boosting benefits of setting aside regular time to read a good book, a newspaper or a magazine. If you suffer from eye strain, the benefits are similar if you listen to audiobooks.

Take action

Set aside at least 15–30 minutes every evening to do some reading. It's a perfect way to unwind, but in a way that is good for you. The ideal time to read your book is in bed, just before you go to sleep, as reading is a much better way to relax and unwind than watching a video, which can disrupt sleep. Switch off your phone, get into bed or find somewhere you won't be disturbed, and lose yourself in a good book. If at any point you feel that you are wasting time on things that aren't real or relevant to daily life, gently focus your mind on the evidence that proves conclusively that reading can significantly improve your brain function and boost your empathy and creativity.

Remember how much you probably enjoyed being read to before you went to sleep when you were a child. Even though you are older now, and you are reading for yourself, your brain hasn't lost its appetite for a really absorbing good-night story. Reading

---

57 Berns, G.S. *et al.* (2013) 'Short- and long-term effects of a novel on connectivity in the brain.' *Brain Connectivity*, 3(6) 590–600.

fiction is probably the best way to start your new reading plan, but it doesn't matter whether you read fiction or non-fiction, just be gently aware that what you absorb or learn while reading can make you smarter and enhance your creativity. In short, reading every day is good for you and stimulates your brain. What is more, it's good for other people too, as there's some research[58] to suggest that people who read regularly may be kinder! In a study, 123 participants were quizzed on their preferences for books and TV. Following this, their interpersonal skills were studied, how they treated other people and to what extent they considered other people's feelings. The study found that people who read more frequently were more likely be empathetic and friendly than those who preferred TV!

Note: This act of self-kindness lays the foundation and prepares the path ahead for ways 26–40, being kinder online.

Evening – Way 23: Be quiet

Just as the first few hours of your day are your power hours when you set the tone for the day ahead, the hours before you go to sleep are equally potent. I call them your golden hours because what you do for yourself each evening can help you to enjoy a refreshing sleep and ensure you wake up energised and in a positive frame of mind. An increasing body of research[59] suggests that regular alone time is remarkably life-enhancing.

---

58 www.kingston.ac.uk/news/article/1856/22-may-2017-kingston-university-students-research-into-fiction-habits-and-personality-types-reveals-reading-may-make-us.

59 Thomas, V.D. (2017) *How to Be Alone: An Investigation of Solitude Skills.* UC Santa Cruz. ProQuest ID: Thomas_ucsc_0036E_11275. Merritt ID: ark:/13030/m59s6mb9. Retrieved from https://escholarship.org/uc/item/4gm0c2vq

Solitude is strongly linked to creativity and inner peace but, despite this, many people associate solitude with feeling blue or missing out. This way to be kind to yourself shows you that nothing could be further from the truth. Being happy in your own company is extremely liberating and empowering. There is great power and peace in solitude, and ensuring you set aside some quiet time every evening when the day is nearly done, away from everyone and everything, is one of the kindest gifts you can give to yourself.

Take action

Every evening, be sure to spend at least ten minutes, preferably longer, alone. Be sure to switch your phone to silent so only emergency calls can come through to it. You can use this quiet time to daydream or simply to let your mind wander.

If you live in a busy home, it may not be easy to find alone time, so tell the other members of your household you need a few minutes to yourself and ask them not to disturb you. Try taking a long bath or shower or simply putting in your headphones. If weather permits, you might like to go for a short walk. The important thing is that you are alone and, most important of all, that you switch off your phone. If you live alone, you may feel that you get more than enough solitary time already but, even if this is the case, you can still benefit from a period of quiet away from your phone and the noises and distractions of daily life.

If you experience feelings of anxiety surrounding the idea of being totally alone because you are used to being with other people all the time, this is perfectly natural. In your quiet period, just observe and don't judge your feelings. Even if your alone time feels uncomfortable at first, you will still be gaining the proven benefits of solitude, which can bring greater feelings of self-worth and confidence in the days ahead. You may even come to cherish your time spent alone. Remind yourself that you are choosing to take this time out. Solitude is not the same as loneliness, which is feeling that something is missing in your life. Choosing solitude is giving yourself time to discover your rich inner depth and explore your personal identity and direction.

Evening – Way 24: Write it up

Writing a journal at the end of each day can help you understand yourself and your day better. It can also be cathartic and a catalyst for creativity. You may already do a lot of updates about yourself and what is happening in your life on social media but – let's be honest here – are you posting for yourself or for others? Are you saying what you really think and feel or trying to impress?

A journal is a place where you can be uncensored and totally honest. Although the wave of activism and anti-racism has created an important and long overdue shift, when it comes to your personal or real feelings and thoughts you probably aren't likely to share these in your newsfeed, but you can in your secret journal. Research[60] indicates that keeping a daily journal can ease stress and help us make sense of our lives. It has been shown to improve clarity and perspective, help us achieve goals and even boost immunity. Writing a journal is something kind and empowering you can do for yourself every day.

Writing utilises both the logical and creative parts of your brain, allowing you to use all your brainpower to understand yourself better. And ending your day with a journal entry is an opportunity for you to feel you did the best you could, creating momentum for the following day. You can learn and grow from

---

60 Murray, B. (2002) 'By helping people manage and learn from negative experiences, writing strengthens their immune systems as well as their minds.' *American Psychological Association*, 33(6) 54.

your reflections about your day. It also reminds you that there is a part of you that is sacred and private and just for you. It is the part that doesn't need validation from others. Writing a journal connects you directly to your inner strength.

Take action

You need a journal or a blank notebook and pen for this. Although writing by hand is recommended because it is more immediate, you can keep a journal on your phone or laptop if you prefer to write it digitally. If time is limited, you can record voice notes on your phone.

Simply set aside a few minutes to note not so much the events of your day, but your thoughts and feelings about them. As you write think about what the day taught you and what you might want to do better tomorrow. Write down any creative thoughts you have. If you struggle with this, try referring to yourself in the third person and remember that this journal is private, just for you, so you don't need to put a positive spin on everything. The transformative power of journal writing lies in the honesty. It helps you explore the shadows and, by so doing, find light within yourself.

Your journal has nothing to do with anybody else. It's a safe place for you to express yourself. Write in it every day.

Evening – Way 25: Record your dreams

The final act of kindness towards yourself is arguably the most powerful. Just as your day of self-kindness began with a feeling of gratitude, your day needs to end that way too, however tough or challenging your day has been. By topping and tailing your day with feelings of gratitude, you are well on your way to making being thankful your natural or default position.

Science[61] has proven that feeling more grateful can make you feel happier, healthier and more positive. When participants in a study were asked to write a few sentences each week about things they were grateful for, after ten weeks they were far happier and more optimistic than participants in the study who were asked to write about things that made them unhappy. Another study required participants to write and personally deliver a letter of gratitude to someone and this boosted their happiness score. And studies on couples showed that those who expressed gratitude towards each other regularly were happier than those who expressed concerns. It truly is hard to feel negative when you end the day with an attitude of gratitude, and the good news is this also increases your chances of having amazing dreams. Drifting off into the land of sleep with the mindset that miracles can happen will often bring you vivid and creative dreams. The symbols in our dreams are a gift from our unconscious mind to help us face our fears and make sense of what is going on in our waking life. Research[62] has shown that recalling your dreams is beneficial for your holistic wellbeing because when you dream your unconscious gets an opportunity to help you work through and make sense of emotions and events happening in your waking life.

Take action

Every night, as you are getting ready for bed, reflect on the benefits of self-compassion, such as inner peace, increased chances of achieving your goals and a better relationship with yourself. Doing this, perhaps while you treat yourself to a warm bath or drink a cup of relaxing herbal tea, will make it easier for you to continue being kind to yourself every day, when times are both good and challenging.

---

61 www.health.harvard.edu/healthbeat/giving-thanks-can-make-you-happier.
62 https://greatergood.berkeley.edu/article/item/why_your_brain_needs_to_dream.

Then, when you are ready for bed, be sure to place a pen and a notepad beside your bed, so that when you wake up in the morning you can immediately write down your dreams. You may think you don't dream, but you do – you just don't recall your dreams. They fade from memory as soon as you wake up. But if you jot them down before you get up or do anything, you won't forget them. Every dream can be a rich source of insight and creativity for you to explore, interpret and reflect on, so it's important to get into the habit of writing them down each morning. Your dream journal can then become as cathartic, beneficial, revealing and enlightening as your private journal (see Way 24).

As you place your head on your pillow and close your eyes, let your mind focus on what you have to be grateful for and then say the words 'thank you' out loud or in a whisper. However difficult your day has been, there is always something to be grateful for, like your health, the love of people and animals in your life, the beauty of the night sky or just the fact that you are breathing, because life is the most precious gift of all. Counting your blessings is an act of great kindness to yourself, a way of ending your day on your own terms and a wonderful way to encourage peaceful sleep and sweet dreams.

CHAPTER 3

15 WAYS TO BE KINDER ONLINE

'In a world where you can be anything, be kind.' Anonymous

The consequences of the 2020 pandemic have forced people who had previously avoided or minimalised virtual communication to embrace the internet. Indeed, without the power of the internet, the isolation and sense of loss would have felt unbearable. Now more than ever, the world needs the internet to keep us all connected and to help us survive. However, just as there is a light and dark side to everything, the internet is no exception.

Cyber-bullying, trolling or flaming is the terrible price humanity is paying for this wonderful resource. There are so many disturbing reports of people experiencing deep depression and anxiety because of cyber-bullying, or because personal details have been exposed online, sometimes costing people their reputations, livelihoods, savings or even lives.

It seems obvious to say that politeness and kindness online are just as important as they are in real life, but the truth is that many people think of the internet as a place of escapism and fantasy. What happens there isn't real or isn't to be taken seriously, so they can comment and remain anonymous.

But the internet *is* real. What you say and do virtually matters greatly. Indeed, it could be argued that it matters more than what you do in your daily life because once you make a statement online, in the majority of cases it is recorded for eternity. Even if you delete it there is a chance that somebody else has kept a record. It's an alarming thought, but it is also the truth that our virtual footprints will survive even our own deaths as a record of the kind of people we are.

We all need to come to terms with the surreal truth that online communication has a reality of its own. Just as research shows that kind people tend to be happier, being kind online can have the same impact. The internet is a world of infinite possibility. You can be anonymous. You can showcase your talents, discover new ones, make exciting connections, learn about everyone and everything and dream impossible dreams. While this potential is wildly exciting, it can also make it much harder to control your emotions and be as self-aware and in control of your words and actions as you are in real life.

So, the next 15 ways to be kind focus entirely on being kinder online. The first five ways continue where the previous section left off by encouraging you to be as kind as possible in the way you treat yourself or present your image online. The remaining ten ways offer a simple introduction to internet etiquette when interacting with other people online. It's something that perhaps should be taught in schools from an early age because, like it or not, we now live in a world where what we say and do online matters as much as in real life.

Yourself online – Way 26: Set the right profile

In the world today, where your online presence is given great importance, your profile picture – whether for social media, groups or professional sites – matters greatly. Your profile says a great deal about you. It's the first thing everybody sees and the instant impression, whether justified or not, that others form of you begins there. Research[63] shows that the smallest detail in a person's profile picture can influence another's decision about whether they want to interact with them or not. Indeed, it seems that we make a decision about someone from their photo in less than one tenth of a second! The biography or text accompanying your photo isn't nearly as impactful. There's really no way around it. Your profile photo is a big deal.

Take action

Take a good long look at your profile picture. Of course, you want to present yourself in the best light, but does it reveal your true self? Is it honest? Is this someone you would want to get to know better or work with?

The aim of this exercise is not to make you overly conscious about your appearance, but to encourage you to spend time considering the impact your profile photo may have on someone who has never met you. Spend as much time on getting it right as you would if you met someone new for the first time in person.

If you feel your photo captures your essence and presents you in an honest, positive and kind light, that's fine. But, if you feel it could be misunderstood, do yourself a big favour and make a change. There's a whole emerging science[64] of advice that you can discover online about creating an appealing profile picture: it seems that a laughing smile showing teeth and slightly scrunched eyes (avoid hats or sunglasses), and a head-and-shoulders shot with a bright background works best. For women, looking directly at the camera is considered most genuine, whereas for men the preference is looking slightly away.

---

63 Todorov, A. *et al.* (2014) 'Misleading first impressions: Different for different facial images of the same person.' *Psychological Science*, 25(7) 1404–1417.

64 www.pnas.org/content/pnas/111/32/E3353.full.pdf.

Photos that look natural and believable are always viewed most positively. If you don't think it matters, remind yourself of what research is showing. You don't have to look like a supermodel or an Instagram influencer, but you do need to look like someone who is authentic, helpful and engaging. It's worth taking the time to ensure that your profile picture be as kind to you as possible without looking forced. And do update your profile at least every few years too, as people want to know what you look like now, not 15 years ago. Constantly changing your profile picture can be just as disorientating, so find a happy medium.

Remember, in the online world, when it comes to forging meaningful personal connections, truth and authenticity do count more than spin, even though it can often appear otherwise.

Yourself online – Way 27: Check out your friends

For most people, strong social connections are an essential ingredient in a happy, healthy and fulfilling life. One of the kindest things you can do for yourself is surround yourself with people who 'get' you and support you. But what about online connections? There is research[65] to show that they can have a positive impact, perhaps even increasing lifespan, but there is more convincing evidence[66] to suggest that the impact of online 'friends' can be detrimental.

Online friendship can be very seductive. Everybody wants to be your friend and it can feel very flattering. When I first dipped my toe into social media, I was so touched that people wanted

---

65 Hobbs, W. *et al.* (2016) 'Online social integration is associated with reduced mortality risk.' *Proceedings of the National Academy of Sciences*, 113(46) 12980–12984.

66 Vanman, E. (2018) 'Interpersonal Relationships in the Digital Age/The burden of online friends: The effects of giving up Facebook on stress and well-being.' *The Journal of Social Psychology*, 158(4) 496–508.

me to be their 'friend' I accepted every invitation not thinking to check out who these new 'friends' were – I just trusted, and my friendship tally soon climbed into the thousands. But a year later I was dismayed to find my face appearing on profiles of pro-gun lobbyists and other bizarre scenarios for a spiritual author. Repulsed, I went on a virtual friend cull until my personal profile reflected people I cared about or admired.

I also let my personal profile remain dormant and posted author updates on my business platforms instead. I kept my personal life private, with phone calls, texts or meetings. I know I'm doing the right thing here, as a recent study[67] stressed the health- and happiness-boosting advantage of face-to-face interaction over online connection. So 'unfriending' on my socials was an act of kindness to myself online.

Take action

Our hearts can tell the difference between what is fake and what is real, even if our heads can't. So, this way to be kind to yourself encourages you to go through your social media carefully and take a long, hard look at your friends and followers.

Who are the people you interact most with online and is the interaction positive? If it isn't, unfriend them. And once you have looked at your closest online companions, cast your eye over all the others. Don't allow your desire to look or appear popular override your authenticity.

Of course, if you are an online influencer, blocking fans isn't possible or advised, as it is your business, but you can still take a look at the people you interact with personally or befriend online.

---

67 Liam, M. *et al.* (2017) 'All you need is Facebook friends? Associations between online and face-to-face friendships and health.' *Frontiers in Psychology*, 8, 68.

In a recent survey,[68] people with hundreds of friends online said that on average only around four were people they felt close to.

If you struggle with the concept of unfriending and want to keep lots of online 'friends', the best and kindest advice to yourself is to regard them as passers-by or casual acquaintances instead of friends you can trust in a crisis.

Yourself online – Way 28: Clear your digital footprint

Every time you go online and surf or search, you leave behind a digital footprint that is detected by interested parties who then feel they have a right to reach out to you with their products, beliefs or points of view. Fortunately, awareness[69] of the digital footprint we create each time we go online is steadily growing, but there is still a long way to go before the message gets through loud and clear.

You can choose what you do and don't want to see, and your choices are reflected back to you in a virtual world of your own creation. This is empowering and affirming but bear in mind that your own filtering of information can have an impact on what appears in your newsfeed.

If you have followed Way 26 hopefully your social media pages are filled with messages from real friends or showcase things or people you are really interested in. And if you are responsible and authentic in your online surfing, the updates and messages that reach you will be in line with that. Going online will feel safe and comforting. The opposite, of course, could be true if you haven't been discriminating in your online choices.

68 www.telegraph.co.uk/news/science/science-news/12108412/Facebook-
    users-have-155-friends-but-would-trust-just-four-in-a-crisis.html.

69 www.researchgate.net/publication/331029914_An_examination_
    of_digital_footprint_awareness_and_digital_experiences_of_higher_
    education_students.

Take action

As well as encouraging you to be selective about your online friendships and associations, this way to be kinder to yourself online urges you to monitor the groups you visit and the places you surf. And if you don't want to be flooded with constant advertising, junk and spam, and your personal details to be harvested, be careful about sharing your personal details online. Ensure that your security settings are constantly updated and in place.

Stop and think before you click on any link. Clear your internet history often. Consider whether the site, group, personal profile or website you are about to land on is in line with your values. Remember, as the world moves forward, the online world is – whether we like it or not – taking on a reality all of its own. Your digital footprints are starting to matter as much as the footprints you leave on real sand.

Of course, curiosity is important and the danger with staying in your online comfort zone is the same as it is in real life – you won't be exposed to other points of view. However, what I am talking about here is not narrow-mindedness – indeed, I would encourage you to be open-minded and connect with people who have different points of view to your own – but your values, your integrity. If something online is clearly not in line with your values, the new rule of thumb is to ask yourself if you would be happy in your waking life to spend time or invest your energy there. If the answer is no, don't let curiosity get the better of you. Do yourself and your digital footprint a big favour and navigate away.

Yourself online – Way 29: Beat temptation

If you are like most people these days, you are probably using social media or texting apps and messaging for either your work or your personal life. But don't be surprised if they become addictive – and when a text alert, message, email or update arrives, you can't resist dropping everything to instantly check it.

Studies[70] show that the lure of online interaction is not in your head. It is down to two chemicals in your brain that are released every time you post or receive a virtual post, message or update. These two chemicals are dopamine and oxytocin. Dopamine is a pleasure chemical released when we want something and oxytocin is known as the 'cuddle' or feel-good hormone, released when we fall in love. No surprise then that an incoming text, tweet or email has an irresistible draw, with one study[71] showing it is as addictive as nicotine and alcohol.

People also feel better about themselves when others react positively to what they post on social media. The 'like' or thumbs-up button is a powerful psychological tool.

Take action

Becoming aware of the addictive quality of social media, texting apps and that 'like' button is the first and most important step. Once you are aware, you realise that social media should complement, not dictate, your life. You are the one in control here. Silence those alerts and set aside a time to review them when it's convenient for you. The majority of alerts are not urgent – even though the designers use manipulative tricks to make you feel you can't live without them. But you really can. Remember, these apps and platforms are businesses that need users. It truly isn't essential to see that funny cat meme right now!

---

70 www.inman.com/next/on-what-social-media-does-to-your-brain.

71 Dwyer, R. *et al.* (2016) 'Addicting via hashtags: How is Twitter making addiction? *Sage Journal*, 43(1) 79–97. Article first published online: 23 March 2016.

Recent research[72] suggests that people with greater self-esteem and sense of purpose in life do not have their responses or moods dictated by the whims of a 'like' button. So, one of the kindest things you can do for yourself online is to remember that your self-esteem and what you are doing with your life matter far more than anything on apps and social media.

From now on, loosen the addictive hold of that 'like' button. When you post, do so because something matters or reveals the honest, authentic you. Posting simply to chase 'likes' is totally meaningless. And if you post something about yourself and nobody likes it, it really doesn't matter. Think about it – when a post about a psychic goldfish gets more 'likes' than a profound quote, why does it matter how many 'likes' you get?

If your heart gives your post the thumbs up, that's all the kind validation you need.

Yourself online – Way 30: Sign off

One of the kindest things we can do for ourselves is to regularly sign off from social media and from screens in general. Life isn't nourished by a screen but by what we dream, feel, say and, above all, do in the real world. Indeed, studies[73] have shown that as many as one in three of us feels dissatisfied with our lives after visiting social media sites. The endless emphasis on friends, 'likes' and followers fosters feelings of envy and low self-esteem.

Previously, one of the ways to be kinder to yourself encouraged you not to check your phone first thing (see Way 7) and this way

---

72 Burrow, A.L. *et al.* (2016) 'How many likes did I get? Purpose moderates links between positive social media feedback and self-esteem.' *Journal of Experimental Social Psychology*, 69, 232–236.

73 Shensa, A. *et al.* (2018) 'Social media use and depression and anxiety symptoms: A cluster analysis.' *American Journal of Health Behavior*, 42(2) 116–128.

to be kinder to yourself online encourages you to keep away from your phone and the constant demands of social media by making sure you spend more time signed off and actually living, rather than online just talking about it.

Take action

The only way to understand how much control phones and screens have over you is to set aside regular time each day to operate without them. For at least an hour, preferably longer, sign off social media and switch your phone to silent or call-only. Then, use that time to plan, tidy up, create, cook, garden, walk in nature, dream or *do* something else. (If loved ones need to contact you during your sign-off period, tell them to call you.)

You may well feel a strong urge to turn your devices back on but resist and simply notice that urge. You don't need to act on it. Remind yourself that you are putting your real, rather than virtual, life centre stage. And it's about time. Sometimes the only resolution to a frozen computer screen is to switch it off, wait a few moments and then reboot it. That's what you are doing now. You are taking time out to restart your creativity and return with a fresh perspective.

At the end of the hour, reflect on how powerful it felt to spend time away from all those online demands and more on experiencing your real life. You don't have to stop there. The benefits may be so strong that you wish to extend that hour to two or have a set time each evening, say after 7 p.m., when you sign off completely until the next morning. You can experiment with leaving or taking extended social media holidays and keep the momentum going by unsubscribing from apps and email subscriptions you don't need. Or use an internet tool to restrict your time online, such as Freedom or SelfControl. How about spending an entire day offline or choosing the life-changing option of a call-only mobile?

The more you make the decision to sign off on a regular basis, the more addicted to living and loving your own life you become.

Others online – Way 31: Comment and share with love

The online world, and social media in particular, hosts a lot of negativity. Research[74] shows that people are more likely to be unkind online rather than face-to-face because the anonymity limits their self-awareness. In addition, their comments and re-actions reflect what they already believe or feel *before* they see or read something online. In other words, what they are saying is about them and not you. I've learned not to take online trolling personally, but unpleasantness is never easy to deal with. As a rule of thumb, the best way to deal with it is to remain polite and if that doesn't work to disengage.

Although there is negativity, there is also a tremendous amount of kindness online. The following ten ways to be kind are all sug-gestions to help you become a force for compassion in all of your online interactions. Commit to them daily and by so doing you can help create a much-needed wave or ripple effect of kindness trending online.

Being kind online is simple and quick to do, and with so many of us online these days it can have a hugely positive impact. Nowhere is this truer than when commenting and sharing the posts, blogs or work of others.

Take action

How many times have you read or admired a post or blog but not stopped to say thank you to its creator? Chances are you've

---

74 https://greatergood.berkeley.edu/article/item/scientific_reasons_to_be_
nice_online.

done this many times and that's understandable as we all lead busy lives but, the next time you are online and you read, see or listen to something that speaks to you in a positive way, do take a minute to leave a comment.

Commenting can really help the person posting, blogging or podcasting, as it sends a message their work mattered to you. In addition, research[75] on news sites has also shown that comments on posts or blogs can influence how other people react. It's the same with podcasts – leaving a review can help the podcaster get wider circulation and also give them the motivation to keep going. I'm always deeply grateful whenever people leave a review for my White Shores podcast, as it is a labour of love that can be very time-consuming, and knowing people are listening and it's informing or inspiring them means the world.

Of course, you may also come across posts and blogs online that you strongly disagree with, and I encourage you to comment on them, too, but in a polite and constructive way. If you find yourself condemning them or being negative, it's best to say nothing at all. It's so easy to criticise, see the negative and point out flaws, but if someone puts themselves out there with good intentions, there is nothing to be gained from putting them down unnecessarily. Remember the golden online rule: only say what you would be prepared to say to someone's face if they were sitting in front of you, instead of being invisible in the ether.

And just as commenting positively or constructively can be a very kind thing to do, so can sharing posts and blogs to your contacts or platforms. Promoting other people not only supports them but says a great deal about how kind and generous a person you are.

---

75 Anderson, A. *et al.* (2014) 'The "Nasty Effect:" Online incivility and risk perceptions of emerging technologies.' *Journal of Computer Mediated Information*, 19(30) 373–387.

Others online – Way 32: Give your hearts

Whenever we engage in face-to-face communication, we unconsciously mimic facial expressions to register our empathy. This is known as emotional contagion. When you are invisible online this emotional contagion is replaced by the wonder of emojis, those familiar thumbs-up, heart or frowning icons. It is estimated that around 90 per cent of people use emojis as a form of communication when online, and billions of them are sent each day. It seems that emoji use is a common theme[76] among social media influencers, and people tend to think people who use emojis are generally friendlier and more approachable.

However, emoji use is not appropriate in all settings, and you should exercise caution in business settings but, in all areas of life, the more you can use your heart emoji, the better. When others post, in the great majority of cases, they are doing so because they wish to reveal something about themselves. They want other people to get to know them better. They are making themselves vulnerable by doing so and therefore, when someone reacts positivity, this is going to make the person who posted feel comforted and validated. If you know the person you are 'hearting', this adds closeness to your relationship but, even if you don't know the person, it gives them a welcome confidence boost.

Take action

From now on, when you go online, I want you to throw caution to the wind and use your heart emoji with wild abandon. Avoid the negative on your social media feeds, seek out the positive and spread love hearts, not hate.

You may wonder why I haven't suggested the 'like' emoji or button here. There is a reason for that. The 'like' emoji or button

---

76 https://digiday.com/careers/year-emojis-5-charts.

is a cool thumbs-up sign, but it can sometimes seem a little half-hearted. It says that your thoughts have been engaged by the post, whereas the heart button signifies that what you have seen, heard or read has touched you. It's a much greater compliment to know that something you posted or wrote has made someone feel emotion, as well as made them think. Of course, a 'like' icon is always welcome but, if you can add in a heart, so much the better because the world always needs more hearts.

There will be times when you feel the need to use the frown, anger or crying emojis, but use them with caution and when you do, explain why. Perhaps it is because a post has highlighted an issue you feel passionate about or are campaigning against. And remember that it is easy to misinterpret emojis. For example, when people post about the death of a loved one – should you post a heart emoji to show that you loved that person or a crying emoji to show that you are sad they have gone? Whenever there is room for misinterpretation, use your emoji with care and explain why you have used it, so as not to cause unnecessary confusion or unintended upset.

Others online – Way 33: Radiate animal magic

While there is no doubt that social media can trigger insecurities and be a hotbed of negativity, it can also be a place that unites us. It's a place where, if you are feeling low, you can receive support from people you care about as well as people you don't know. If you have ever received and benefited from an avalanche of virtual empathy, you will understand the very real healing power of virtual empathy and connection.

So, if you ever get an opportunity to show you understand or relate to someone who is posting and clearly going through a rough time in their lives, be sure to do so. Recognise their struggle and the shared human experience they are going through. Understand that they are coming from a position of pain, and show compassion.

People who empathise with humans often have a deep connection with animals, too. If you have ever wondered why animal posts and videos often go viral, research by journalists[77] has highlighted a possible explanation, which is that posts about animals not only showcase the creatures' appeal but also human nature at its finest. These posts show humans caring for, rescuing and connecting with empathy to animals. So, if you want to remind others of their shared humanity and deep capacity for compassion and kindness, join in with spreading the animal love online. The more empathy is revealed openly in the virtual world, the more it will cross over into real life.

Take action

At its best, social media can give a huge platform to what is good in the world. It is about noticing that good in others as well as in ourselves, and then sharing that goodness to as big an audience as possible, so those watching can also recognise the good in themselves.

Focus your precious energy on the upsides of shared connection and empathy and, if negativity strikes or you simply want to spread some positivity and connect with others, post a cute animal video in which you see someone interacting with empathy and heart to another species. There are stacks out there to delight you. I especially recommend, as a starting point, vintage footage of Christian the Lion, who was born in captivity and purchased by Australian John Rendall and Anthony 'Ace' Bourke from Harrods department store in London in 1969. A few years later he was reintroduced to the African wild by a conservationist called George

---

77 www.gq.com/story/buzzfeed-beastmaster-profile-march-
    2014?currentPage=1.

Adamson. A year after releasing Christian into the wild, Rendall and Bourke decided to go looking for him to see whether Christian was thriving or not and also whether the lion would remember them. They were delighted when Christian most certainly did – as did the two lionesses who were with him – and the footage of their reunion is unbelievably beautiful.

Note: If in your search you come across any images of animal cruelty, flag them up and report them immediately. Positive change can only happen when kind people speak up.

Others online – Way 34: Brush up your email etiquette

The concept that we are all connected is not just a spiritual philosophy, it has become a mobile phone advertising slogan and a reality, given we can instantly connect to each other via online platforms and, of course, good 'old-fashioned' email. Even though texting and messaging reign supreme in the virtual world, emails have never gone out of fashion and remain the preferred way for many businesses, organisations and individuals to communicate. An email doesn't have the formality of a mailed letter, but it does have the power to spread kindness and make anyone reading it feel better.

These days, email management can be time-consuming, and research[78] has shown that the expectation to constantly monitor and respond to emails all day, every day is having a negative impact on wellbeing. Sorting through and responding to emails can feel like a chore and worse if the emails a person receives are confusing

---

78 Becker, W.J. *et al.* (2018) 'Killing me softly: Electronic communications monitoring and employee and spouse well-being.' *Academy of Management best paper proceedings*, no 1.

or disrespectful. That's why taking care with your email etiquette is a truly kind thing to do and can make someone's day easier.

Take action

Here are some ways you can email with kindness and not only show people you respect them but also encourage them to respond in kind to you.

First, pay attention to the subject line. Leaving it blank or cryptic can create confusion. Be sure to greet them by starting with 'Hello...', 'Dear...' or 'Hi...' and use their name if you know it. Not doing so is the equivalent of shouting, 'Hey, you' across a room. It's rude.

Take your time, writing clearly and concisely – people are busy, so get to the point. Also consider whether what you are sending is necessary, as most people's inboxes these days are clogged. Once sent, your email can't be deleted by you, so check that what you have written isn't something you will regret later. You should also reread it to make sure you have not made any spelling or grammar errors. Above all, spell the recipient's name right. This is simply showing them courtesy.

You may feel that this way to be kinder online is not a big deal, but it truly is. Making someone else feel respected when they read your email can make a big difference. And on that note of kindness and respect, there is something else you can do that has tremendous power. You can send emails to people you don't know but admire. This is not stalking. You are simply saying 'Well done' or 'I respect you' or 'I enjoyed what you did or said' to someone. The majority of emails we receive are mundane, so getting one that simply pays a compliment can be wonderful. It's easy to forget that everyone – however confident they may appear – needs motivating and congratulating now and again to give them a welcome boost.

Others online – Way 35: Zooming in

Even if you hadn't fully embraced video calls, whether via Zoom, Google, Skype or another platform, before, you will likely have been encouraged to experiment with them during the lockdown. Indeed, social distancing has altered the way people communicate dramatically, forcing even those who suffer from phone anxiety[79] or who are internet phobic to stay in touch and embrace online connectivity.

Video calls are an effective, intimate way to connect with people when you can't see them in person. Research[80] shows that face-to-face online meetings are far more likely to increase feelings of empathy[81] than emails or phone calls. However, this can have its pitfalls. It's easy to offend or upset people without realising it, so here is some important video-call etiquette.

Take action

The kindest thing to do before a video call is to check that the people you want to speak to are happy to go ahead. You may feel comfortable chatting face-to-face, but another person may not for many reasons. Perhaps they don't feel they look good on camera, or their house or office is a mess, or maybe they simply want to keep a distance. Their reason for not wanting to video-call you is not your concern. Alternatively, you could start with a voice call and then ask them if they want to switch to video. Whatever you decide to do, be sure not to surprise them by video-calling without warning or suddenly switching on your video and putting them on the spot. They could feel tremen-

---

79 www.bbc.com/worklife/article/20200408-coronavirus-how-lockdown-helps-those-who-fear-the-phone.

80 www.washingtonpost.com/sf/brand-connect/hilton/the-science-of-being-there.

81 Cole, J. (2001) 'Empathy needs a face.' *Journal of Consciousness Studies,* 8(5–7) 51–68.

dous pressure to switch on their video too, if they can see you but you can't see them.

If you both agree to video-call, test your technology before-hand. It is disrespectful to keep somebody waiting because you haven't got the latest update or can't figure out how it works. It goes without saying that looking as nice as you can and ensuring that the setting you are calling from is pleasant helps as much in establishing bonds as it would if you met that person in real life. In much the same way, complimenting that person and asking how they are can help put them at ease.

Try to minimise distractions because the person you are talking to will see you being distracted. This can have the same diminish-ing effect as when you meet someone at a party or a social event and while talking to you, they keep glancing over your head to see who else is there they might want to talk to. It also helps to know where your camera lens is so you can look into it because then the other person will see you looking at them directly rather than at some random point.

Others online – Way 36: Be an 'upstander'

Standing up for kindness and positivity online takes courage but being silent in the face of bullying or unpleasantness can contrib-ute to the problem. This way to be kinder online isn't asking you to hunt out negativity, take the moral high ground or interfere in things you know nothing about, but it *is* asking you to call a spade a spade. If, unfortunately, you do experience or witness bullying or unkindness, call it out. The more often we stand up to bullying, the less power it has to destroy hearts and minds.

You only need to reference those tragic stories often reported in the press about people taking their own lives because of cyber-bullying, to understand how important it is for online bullying – also known as flaming or trolling – to be reported. In many cases, loved ones had no idea the person was suffering. For some reason, they felt totally alone and that nobody could support them. So, taking a stand when you witness any kind of cyber-bullying could potentially save lives.

Google's 'Internet Awesome' campaign[82] offers a number of anti-bullying skills for parents and teachers to use to help children and young adults become 'upstanders' – people who intervene online and stand up for the power of spreading kindness.

Take action

There are some proven strategies[83] to help you when you encounter cyber-bullying, because it's not just children and young people who need to be taught how to stand up for kindness online – we all do.

If you notice any trolling when you are personally interacting in a group online or following a conversation, simply call it out. 'That's bullying' or 'What you are saying is unkind' will suffice. There is no need for you to be unpleasant or to get personal, just stick to the facts. Don't become a bully yourself, though.

If the campaign of hatred continues, don't engage any further. Report the incident. Every social media platform or network provides a way for you to report bullying and to remain anonymous if you wish. And reporting is something you can still do if you simply witness unkindness but are not personally involved in the online interaction.

If you can, send a message of support to the victim, who may feel extremely vulnerable and unsupported. The internet becomes a fearful place for them, so the more positive and supportive messages they receive to counteract the negativity, the better.

---

82 https://beinternetawesome.withgoogle.com.

83 Lee, H. (2005) 'Behavioral strategies for dealing with flaming in an online forum.' *The Sociological Quarterly*, 46, 385–403.

*

Note: If you are the target of bullying, take action and don't ever keep it to yourself. Ask friends and loved ones to support you and to report the bully. As hard as it can be, keep a sense of perspective and remember that when people target you unfairly, they are really talking to themselves. They deserve your pity, not your fear. Someone who devotes their energy to pulling down others must be very unhappy indeed.

Others online – Way 37: Hit subscribe

JustGiving[84] is one of many online sites that offer you opportunities to participate in online fundraising, donating to charity or a good cause. It's a wonderfully kind and positive community to join, but if you are not in a position to fundraise or donate, there is a free way to support or help good people or causes.

Let's start with individuals. Following or commenting positively about people you admire or want to help really can help their analytics build momentum. Countless experts offer expertise and wisdom for free via their YouTube channels, podcasts and online platforms. If you have a question or want to find out about anything, the chances are when you do an online search you will find someone with insight to offer you. Of course, you do need to be careful not to believe everything you read, see or hear online because there is no quality control. But if you carefully check your sources and use your common sense, you can often get remarkable insight, advice and inspiration online.

Take action

When you do find something helpful online, don't take it for granted but leave a positive comment or review and, if there is an

---

84 www.justgiving.com.

option to hit the subscribe button, do so. It's a free and easy way to say thank you and by so doing continue to spread kindness and positivity online.

When people offer their services or advice for free online, gathering as many subscribers as they can is the only way they can potentially earn some income from what they are doing. Demonstrate your gratitude either by leaving a positive comment or review or, better still, by subscribing. This lets them know that their work, advice or entertainment they are offering is making a difference to you – you value what they are offering.

The same applies for any good causes that you may want to actively support, such as environmentalism, charitable campaigns or human or animal rights issues. Subscribing to these causes and their campaigns online is a highly effective way to help them do their important work. It may not seem like much, but your subscription really can make all the difference. Growing an internet presence isn't easy and they need your support. Every new subscriber, follower, comment, review and 'like' helps, especially if they are setting themselves goals and targets to keep doing their work.

You can also make the decision to only shop online with brands and companies that team up with good causes, or firms promoting diversity.

Others online – Way 38: Share your knowledge

Sometimes the best way to be kinder online is to share what you know or have learned.

You are irreplaceable. What you bring to the world is unique. Over the course of your life you learn and do many amazing things and find your own way to navigate the slings and arrows of fortune. And when you make a discovery or find something that helps you or moves you deeply, sharing that discovery, wisdom or insight with others may just help or inspire them, too.

This way to be kinder online encourages you to post about your own experiences or insights, and to join forums to share your knowledge and reveal what you know about subjects you are passionate about. Your generous sharing might just help, improve or utterly transform someone else's life. You may never know how your life wisdom has impacted others, but the chances are it will because simply reading about what helped another person cope or change their life for the better can be highly motivational.

I know the power of sharing because, over the many years I have been a spiritual writer, I have shared true life stories in my books. The common theme is experiences or sudden insights that have helped people find a silver lining or new way of looking at things to help pull them through times of loss and grief. I have lost count of the number of messages I've received from grateful readers saying these stories comforted them greatly or gave them a brilliant new perspective. There is transformative[85] power in sharing, with research showing that happiness and life satisfaction increase when participants share or discuss their positive experiences with others. So every time you share, you are not just giving yourself a positive affirmation but spreading a message of kindness and generosity online.

Take action

Make a commitment to share things that have helped you solve or overcome problems, made your life easier or simply given you a much-needed boost. You can edit the details so that you only share what you are comfortable with – for example, tips for dealing with stress at work or how you dealt with feelings of sadness following the death of your pet. If you have gained life wisdom

---

85 Lambert, N.M. *et al.* (2013) 'A boost of positive affect: The perks of sharing positive experiences.' *Journal of Personal and Social Relationships*, 30(1) 24–43.

through something you experienced or went through in your life that helped you move forward, the kindest thing to do is not to keep it to yourself but to share it to help others.

And don't stop with your life wisdom, share your knowledge about practical things that have worked for you, too. This can range from beauty and hair care tips to cleaning or gardening advice, to books, movies and artwork that have made an impression and lifted your spirits. If a therapy or treatment or massage has benefited you, talk about it.

As long as the impact on you was positive, tell others about it. You never know who might benefit.

Others online – Way 39: Say good morning and good night

There is something very simple and obvious you can do to help someone you care about start and end their day right if you can't talk to or see them as often as you would like – simply send them a text or a message to bid them good morning or good night.

Sometimes there is no time, or it is not appropriate to phone or video-call someone but sending a text to say 'Good morning' or 'Good night' can be a wonderful kick-start or ending to the recipient's day. Everyone, however introverted, needs human connection, because we humans are social creatures. Getting a 'Good morning' or 'Good night' text can help make someone feel incredibly valued and comforted. It means that first thing when you wake up and last thing at night you are thinking of them and sending them positive vibes.

Increasing numbers of people are living alone these days, so receiving texts like this from family members or friends can be incredibly therapeutic. This is especially the case if someone is elderly. And while on the subject of seniors, if there is an elderly person in your life who is not online because they are fearful of or reluctant to embrace new technology, you may want to offer to teach them the basics. There is a lot of nonsense and darkness online, but there is also a world of infinite possibilities to learn, share and connect to people all over the world. Not to take advantage of that wonderful resource is limiting. Indeed, research[86] has shown that seniors who do embrace the online world are better connected and have higher levels of life satisfaction than those who refuse to move with the times. So, go ahead and teach them what you know – you may both be pleasantly surprised!

Take action

If there is someone you care about, or are concerned about, but for whatever reason it is not possible to talk to them or see them as much as you would like, send them a text first thing in the morning or last thing at night, or both. You can add more to the text if you wish, but a simple 'Good morning, how are you today?' or 'Good night, sweet dreams!' will suffice. You don't even have to invite interaction or a reply. It's a text with no agenda, just to say you care.

You can do this once in a while or more frequently, if you wish. Quantity isn't important here. What matters is the feeling it generates. You are sending this person a text because you genuinely want them to know you are thinking about them and you care.

Others online – Way 40: Spread hashtag kindness

The internet is so much a part of our lives today, and studies[87] show that what happens to us online and what we encounter

---

86 Boz, H. *et al.* (2015) 'Review of internet use and quality of life in the elderly.' *Cypriot Journal of Educational Advice*, 10(3) 182–191.

87 McKenna, K.Y.A. & Bargh, J.A. (2000) 'Plan 9 from cyberspace: The implication of the internet for personality and social psychology.' *Personality and Social Psychology Review*, 4(1) 57–75.

while surfing and going on social media influences our thoughts, feelings, personality, relationships and even our life choices. It would not be an understatement to say that virtual reality today is shaping our lives and our world view. That's why it truly is worth the effort to join in the action to make the online world a kinder and more positive place.

There is a lot of talk about doing random acts of kindness[88] in the real world and the life-changing power of that movement, so take that sentiment to the next level in your digital life. Make sure that, every time you go online, respect for yourself and compassion for others lead the way, whether that is through commenting positively, hitting that heart button, promoting a good cause, posting positive reviews, generously sharing your insights and practical hacks or standing up for kindness whenever there is negativity, and so on.

Whenever you are next online, consciously think of ways that you can help or empower others and choose to make your virtual world a kinder, gentler place. And there is one powerful tool for positive change at your disposal that can really help your mission to spread kindness online gather pace, and that is the mighty hashtag.

Take action

A hashtag is simply a keyword or phrase with the symbol # before it, and this hashtag phrase is then placed in the beginning, middle or at the end of your posts as well as in your comments. These hashtags tie public conversations from different users into a single stream that you can find by searching for a specific hashtag.

We all witnessed the power of the hashtag when #MeToo started to trend in October 2017. It appeared in the wake of the Harvey Weinstein allegations and went on to spark national conversations about sexual harassment as never before, reaching

---

88 www.randomactsofkindness.org/kindness-ideas.

a high point when *Time* magazine named #MeToo activists as persons of the year.

Wouldn't it be wonderful if #kindness could sweep the online world and by so doing never stop impacting both the online and real worlds?

The next time you post about positive things, events, causes or people or simply want to turn the spotlight on kindness, and feel comfortable sharing your post with a wider audience, be sure to make that post public and include #kindness in it. Doing this will make your post visible, significantly increase engagement and connect it to other posts, videos and blogs about the power of kindness online.

In this way, you can play your vital part in helping to change both the real and online worlds for the better by making #kindness go (and hopefully stay) viral.

CHAPTER 4

40 WAYS TO BE KINDER TO OTHERS

Wherever there is a human being, there is an opportunity for kindness. Lucius Seneca

Before you dive into this section, here are some quotes to motivate you to incorporate random ways to be kind into your daily life, and to inspire you to be happier too. Quotes are a great way to spread the beauty of kindness, that never grows old, so feel free to share and share and share them again and again online.

Remember there is no such thing as a small act of kindness. Every act creates a ripple with no logical end. Scott Adams

Sometimes it takes only one act of kindness and caring to change a person's life. Jackie Chan

Do things for people not because of who they are or what they do in return, but because of who you are. Harold S. Kushner

You cannot do a kindness too soon, for you never know how soon it will be too late. Ralph Waldo Emerson

Kindness is more important than wisdom, and the recognition of this is the beginning of wisdom. Theodore Rubin

Always be a little kinder than necessary. J.M. Barrie

The level of our success is limited only by our imagination and no act of kindness, however small, is ever wasted. Aesop

Love and kindness are never wasted. They always make a difference. They bless the one who receives them, and they bless you, the giver. Barbara De Angelis

The next 40 ways to be kinder whisk you away from the virtual world to interactions with others in the real world, although bear in mind that some of them could also apply to calls and on-line interactions. They encourage you to consciously and actively share kindness with others, for the simple reason that whenever kindness is shared, it multiplies.

In many respects, given the racism protests of 2020 and the much-needed global rethink they have inspired, this section is the beating heart of the book. It encourages you to be kinder not just to the people you care about or work with or who share similarities to you but to everyone, regardless of their race, culture, age and status. Kindness to others – seeing someone for who they are, not what they look like – and focusing on our collective beating hearts and what connects rather than separates us is the only and best way forward.

Do be aware, though, that sometimes the best and most empowering way to help someone is to give them the space they need to help themselves. You can tell them you are there to listen and have their back if they need it, but also let them know that you believe in them. If your instinct is always to dive in and try to save the day, knowing when to help and when to step back is an essential life lesson. Sometimes 'helping' can tip over into interference or, worse, encouraging co-dependency.

It sounds paradoxical, but not helping may at times be the optimum way to help or be kind to someone. It encourages them to find their own inner strength. When a child learns to ride a bicycle, there comes a moment when the stabilisers have to come off. The child has to learn through trial and error – and perhaps the odd fall or two – how to balance by themselves. And when that magical moment comes, and they realise they can ride without balance aids, their euphoria is real. Even though you may feel you are helping, robbing someone of the pure joy of doing it by themselves isn't kind.

As a rule of thumb, when it comes to loved ones, friends and colleagues, it's best to wait for them to ask you for help before diving in uninvited if you feel they need help. Obviously, this advice doesn't apply to emergency situations or when someone is dangerously vulnerable. But, in everyday life, respect the boundaries of others at all times and, above all, their own ability to help themselves. That's why the 40 suggestions that follow are all carefully chosen random acts of kindness that are unlikely to offend, cross boundaries or be seen as unwanted interference in any way. They are simply kind things you can do to make others feel good and the world a better place.

Be aware that there may be rare occasions when your acts of kindness towards others may be met with suspicion or hostility. If that happens, try to understand that this has nothing to do with you and everything to do with the other person. Perhaps they are not used to being treated with kindness or perhaps they are simply deeply unhappy, but whatever the reason, don't allow unpleasant responses from others to derail or disenchant you. The overwhelming majority of people will not just appreciate your kindness but bask in the comfort and inspiration it offers them.

And, as well as understanding that sometimes your kindness will not be appreciated and in some instances the kindest way to help is to let go and trust, never allow your kindness to others to be prioritised over kindness to yourself. Self-compassion and compassion for others are linked; they sustain and enhance each other. The kinder you are to yourself, the kinder you are likely to be towards others. And being kinder to others not only helps them feel happier, it has been proven[89] to make you feel happier too, because it triggers a release of feel-good hormones, or the 'helper's high'. There really aren't any downsides. Being kind in all your interactions with others is the happiest way to live and makes a positive and lasting difference in the lives of others.

Being kind has such positive and far-reaching efforts.

Have you been kind enough today?

Others – Way 41: Listen, just listen

Most of us like to think we are good listeners. I used to pride myself on my empathy and ability to listen, but then I launched my own author podcast. Recording interviews with guests required me to listen to them back for editing purposes, before releasing them. It was probably the first time I had heard myself engaged in conversation. I was shocked. I had no idea that I interrupted so much or that my answers, reactions and responses didn't reflect back enough what the person was saying. I found myself feeling frustrated, as it was clear the person I was interviewing was in full flow or about to make or finish a great point, and I was interjecting unnecessarily. It was time to do some soul-searching and to change my approach to conversations.

Study[90] after study has shown that actively listening is a key ingredient for fruitful relationships and a successful life. In our

---

89 Lyubomirsky, S. *et al.* (2005) 'Pursuing happiness: The architecture of sustainable change.' *Review of General Psychology*, 9(2) 111–131.

90 Weger, H. *et al.* (2014) 'The relative effectiveness of active listening in initial interactions.' *International Journal of Listening*, 28(1) 13–31.

busy lives, most of us rarely listen to what others are saying, particularly when someone has a different viewpoint to our own, and struggle to remain silent when others are speaking to us. We aren't fully engaged. We interrupt or lose concentration. This disruption makes the other person feel as if what they say doesn't really matter or isn't interesting enough, and making anyone feel like that – even if it isn't intentional – is not respectful or kind.

Take action

The next time you are in conversation, make a point of fully engaging with the person you are talking to. If you can, look them in the eyes – not directly as that can be off-putting – but enough for them to know you are concentrating on them and what they have to say. Don't think about other things or formulate your reply while the other person is speaking. Be silent. Listen fully. Give that person the gift of your undivided attention. Simply listen to understand that person better, to hear their truth.

Notice what happens when you truly decide to listen. You will notice the calming impact it has on the other person or group you are interacting with. It makes them feel as if what they have to say matters. It can also be transformative for you, as you might learn something new or really important. During the day, make a point of constantly rating yourself as a listener. How engaged were you? Were you empathic? Were you present?

However, don't beat yourself up if you aren't always the best listener. Just make sure that from now on you speak a little less and listen a whole lot more. And if you are a gentle soul who is already a great listener and can rarely get a word in edgeways, be conscious that conversations are a two-way street. Your way to be kind in conversations is to share your truth more and help others understand the joy they can find in active listening.

Remember, if you listen actively you are truly hearing, and if you are truly hearing you are being empathetic and trying to understand where that person is coming from. Understanding is the beginning of hope – hope for a kinder world. Think about that each time you are tempted to speak over someone or interrupt.

Others – Way 42: The space between

We often associate silence in conversation as awkward and do all we can to avoid it at all costs. This next suggestion is another counterintuitive one, as it's encouraging you to incorporate more silences into your conversations. You see, a few seconds of silence give others the space and time to respond and generate a creative response. A study[91] on participants in a writing seminar showed that the teacher used silence to rethink the presentation of the information provided to students and the students exploited silence to revise their writing drafts. Let's consider how transformative silence can be by using a question everyone asks everyone else routinely, although it's the one we are least likely to get an answer to or be given an opportunity to respond properly to: 'How are you?'

How many times has someone asked you how you are and then given you absolutely no space or opportunity to reply? Or to put the shoe on the other foot, how many times have you asked someone how they are as a form of polite greeting rather than a genuine question?

The chances are that if you have been asked countless times how you are, and have constantly found that people aren't really interested in your reply, you respond by simply bouncing the question back with a superficial and equally uninterested, 'I'm well, and how are you?' or something along those lines.

---

91 Mirzae, M. *et al.* (2016) 'Conversation analysis of the function of silence in writing conferences.' *Iranian Journal of Language Teaching Research*, 4(2) 69–86.

A small kind step for one person to take (though it could be a giant step towards spreading kindness in the world if enough people took it) is to give someone a real opportunity to respond when you ask them how they are. If you wait silently you might just find that your conversation becomes deeper and that the other person feels better after interacting with you. Silence is a seriously underrated factor in conversations. We all need to learn to embrace it.

Take action

The next time you find yourself asking someone how they are, resist the urge to move the conversation quickly along. Ask the question then don't say anything at all. Wait at least four or five seconds for them to answer. If they reply, 'I'm fine, how are you?' keep the focus on them and say something like, 'I'll tell you in a moment, but how has your week been?' or something similar. Then stay quiet until they speak. Listen and don't interrupt.

Of course, if they aren't willing to share or don't want to open up, respect their privacy. But ensure you give them ample space and opportunity to tell you how they are first. Don't be surprised if incorporating more silence into your conversations with others takes time to get used to. However, don't give up – keep practising and make a conscious decision to value silence in conversations, no matter how awkward they may initially feel. It is in the silences that you can really connect to another person and they can feel more deeply connected to you.

Others – Way 43: Elevate people

It feels easy and natural to be kind to people who are kind to us. But it's a different matter to be kind to people who are unpleasant. Our instinctive reaction is to retaliate, but this just builds tension and expands the feelings of anger and dislike.

You may not realise it, but your mind is very receptive[92] to suggestions from others because we all have mirror neurons which encourage us to mimic other people even without realising it and so you may unconsciously modify your behaviour to match theirs. One of the kindest things you can do for yourself is to be aware of this unconscious process and not allow others to determine how you feel about yourself and how you behave.

But there is another way to escape the potentially negative influence of others and that is to be kind to them. Scientists have a term for what happens when people unexpectedly experience kindness or see kindness, and that term is 'elevation'. Research[93] shows that elevation motivates people to become kinder themselves, typically making them want to help others and become better people.

But even if elevation does not occur in the other person, responding kindly to unkindness can have an extremely positive impact on you. Your mood and confidence get a huge boost, but you also get a shift in perspective. Being kind gives you a sense of deeper meaning and purpose, because whether the recipient of your kindness is grateful or not, kindness is contagious. Every kind action towards others is helping to change the world for the better and reminds you that you are part of something bigger.

Take action

The next time you encounter unkindness or find yourself caught in a heated argument, choose to retaliate with kindness rather than mirror back what is being thrown at you. This isn't being a pushover or even turning the other cheek, it is responding in the way most beneficial to you and the other person. Even if you dis-

---

92 Michael, R. *et al.* (2012) 'Suggestion, cognition and behaviour.' *Current Directions in Psychological Science*, 21(3) 151–156.

93 Haidt, J. & Keyes, C. (2003) *Flourishing: Positive Psychology and the Life Well-Lived*. Washington DC: American Psychological Association.

agree strongly, acknowledge how the other person is feeling and apologise if you think you have done something wrong. You may just find that it immediately softens the other person's reaction.

When someone is unkind to you, being empathetic (which is not the same as agreeing) and responding with kindness will have an empowering impact for you, and perhaps even on the other person too. Often, the people who are unkind need others to be kind to them the most.

Think back on all those times you got dragged into an argument and how drained you felt afterwards. You may also find – as I do with arguments that I had in the past – that in hindsight, you can't even remember what the argument was about. All you can remember is the tension or the anger. Wouldn't it be better to look back and remember kindness, and the elevation of mood that goes with that, instead?

Others – Way 44: Give compliments

No matter how self-confident someone appears, never underestimate the power of a heartfelt compliment. Research[94] confirms what you already know – compliments can make you feel good about yourself and significantly boost energy and performance. With a few encouraging words you can give someone a much-needed lift for free and boost yourself in the process. Sharing your positivity and seeing the good in others makes you feel great, strengthens your relationships and also makes others want to be around you.

The world is competitive and for this reason many of us feel that success is finite – there is only so much to go around. But nothing could be further from the truth. There is a world of infinite possibility out there. You are not going to limit your own chances of

---

94 Sugawara, S.K. *et al.* (2012) 'Social rewards enhance offline improvements in motor skill.' *PLOS ONE*, 7(11) e48174.

success by congratulating or complimenting others, because there is more than enough success to go around for everyone. If you ever struggle to feel happy for someone else, you need to consider why envy takes over and what you need to do to make your own life more fulfilling. A great place to start is with kindness and selfless congratulation when things go well for others.

It can be hard to be complimentary towards others if you aren't feeling great or happy yourself, but you can and should do it – not just because it is the kind thing to do but because it can also help you. If you are feeling unappreciated, you'll be surprised how much of a lift appreciating others gives you.

Take action

Make a point of paying others more compliments. Don't be insincere or indulge in flattery. That's meaningless. You are going to dish out sincere compliments only. For example, if a loved one empties the dishwasher without prompting, give them a hug and tell them how much you appreciate them. If you think your friend's new hairstyle looks great, tell him or her. Leave a note for the delivery person expressing your gratitude for their prompt service. If a colleague gets a promotion, send them a bunch of flowers to say well done or make a point of congratulating them. Be happy for the success or joy of others.

Be aware that details can give compliments more power, so don't just say, 'Well done!' or 'Congratulations!' but explain why you are saying it. Avoid focusing too much on a person's appearance as that can appear superficial. Reserve most of your compliments for something they have done, their personality traits or life choices.

There are many ways to pay a heartfelt compliment to the people in our lives. Look out for opportunities to lift others up rather than drag them down. And if you do find that compliments are returned to you, don't brush them aside with false modesty, as many of us tend to do. Savour them with good grace. It's a beautiful thing when others notice and appreciate you.

Others – Way 45: Smile and make eye contact

When it comes to kindness, sometimes less is more. It is often the smallest and simplest things that can make the biggest impact. And one of those ordinary yet extraordinary things that you may not feel can make a real difference is the power of a smile with a little eye contact thrown in.

Like kindness, smiling is contagious. If you have ever wondered why, when you see someone else yawn, it makes you want to yawn yourself, what you are experiencing is your mirror neuron system (MNS) at work in your brain.[95] This system encourages you to mirror back the expressions and emotions of others. It also means that when you see someone laugh or smile, you are more likely to laugh or smile yourself. And when you, in turn, smile at someone else, their impulse to smile in empathetic response is more likely to be activated, too.

Along with a smile, eye contact can also have a validating and positive effect on others. It is often said that the eyes are the windows of the soul so when you look into their eyes, what you are doing is truly seeing them. You are connecting to them powerfully.[96] Of course, in certain cultures, eye contact is considered rude and too much eye contact can seem invasive and make someone feel uncomfortable, so you need to know your audience and adapt accordingly. As a rule of thumb, three seconds of eye contact before averting your gaze is considered optimum by psychologists.

95 Basstiansen, J. *et al.* (2009) 'Evidence for mirror systems in emotions.' *Philosophical Transactions of the Royal Society B: Biological Sciences*, 364(1528) 2391–2404.

96 www.bbc.com/future/article/20190108-why-meeting-anothers-gaze-is-so-powerful.

Take action

Make a conscious effort to smile more, not just at loved ones and friends but at colleagues and all the people you interact with each day. You don't have to do a huge toothy smile, a hint of smile will do – the important thing is that you make other people feel that you have noticed them, appreciate them as individuals and are pleased that your paths have crossed.

If your self-esteem is low or you are introverted, you may find smiling frequently challenging. The way forward is to shift the focus away from yourself and onto others. Remind yourself what an empowering and validating gift eye contact and a smile are for others and how smiling is contagious. It's very hard to offend anyone with a genuine smile and a little eye contact, as it makes them feel that their presence is gratefully received.

And if you don't feel like smiling, refer back to Way 10, where you learned that faking a smile with your teeth until your heart joins in will suffice. (Way 10 can also help you start practising your smile, if you feel nervous or shy about showcasing it more.) Remember, everybody has a need to be seen. You really need to experience what a positive difference your smile can make in someone else's day.

Others – Way 46: Say sorry

Nobody is perfect. We all say and do things we regret but, more often than not, we make the situation worse by trying to shift blame or make excuses for our behaviour. We feel that apologising makes us appear weak, but nothing could be further from the truth. It takes courage to apologise. It shows others that you are willing to be honest, accept responsibility and make yourself vulnerable. A sincere apology[97] fosters connection and can be

---

97 Engel, B. (2002) *The Power of an Apology*. Wiley.

emotionally healing and empowering to the recipient. It shows them your respect and empathy; it makes them feel better.

It's easy on days when things aren't going well or when we feel stressed to snap or vent and unintentionally upset or offend others, both loved ones and those we don't know at all. For example, perhaps you have been rude to a delivery person who unintentionally delivered a parcel to your address by mistake. Sometimes you may not get a chance to apologise when you have been rude or thoughtless, but this way to be kind encourages you to make 'sorry' one of your favourite words.

Take action

Whenever you notice that you have said or done something you regret or made a mistake, own it. Take responsibility by going out of your way to say sorry and ask forgiveness, as research[98] shows that this is the most effective way to apologise. Don't qualify your apology with a 'but', make excuses or try to blame someone or something else. 'I was wrong and I am sorry. I hope you can forgive me' will suffice. Notice how light you feel after saying sorry, and how it makes the person you have wronged feel better about themselves.

If you notice yourself resisting saying sorry, ask yourself why you are not accepting responsibility for your words and actions. Remember, it is not a sign of vulnerability to apologise and admit your mistakes but a sign of real character, courage and integrity.

Of course, you should not apologise if you genuinely feel you have done nothing wrong. (If this is the case, you could say something like, 'I'm sorry you feel that way,' as this might help to build bridges when someone is being unreasonable.) However, if

---

98 Lount, R. *et al.* (2016) 'An exploration of the structure of effective
      apologies.' *Negotiation and Conflict Management Research*, 9(2) 177–196.

you know that your words or actions were less than kind, admit it and say sorry.

And if there are people you have offended in your past but never apologised to, seize the moment. Reach out to them if you can and let them know you accept responsibility and are sorry. They may or may not decide to forgive you, but what someone else does is out of your control. What is in your control is your ability to choose to do the right and kind thing, both for yourself and for the other person involved.

Others – Way 47: Send healing

'Sorry' is a powerful word. However, it isn't always possible to apologise to a person you have offended or tell someone how much you care about them. Perhaps that person won't speak to you or you don't know how to contact them or be of help. If that's the case you may feel powerless, but there is still something mighty kind that you can do for them, which you may not have thought about before. You can pray for them or send them healing and positive thoughts.

It feels comforting, doesn't it, when someone says that you are in their prayers? Even if you are not religious or spiritual, part of you senses their good intentions and positive energy towards you. There might just be a reason why it feels so comforting, as although the research is disputed and ongoing there is rising interest in the role of prayer in healing, with some schools of nursing studies[99] suggesting that patients who know they are being prayed for have reduced anxiety and faster healing times. Of course, there could be other factors at play – and any research on the power of prayer is controversial because it involves measuring something

---

99 Simão, T.P. *et al.* (2016) 'The effect of prayer on patients' health: Systematic literature review.' *Religions*, 7(1) 11.

unseen – but whether there is healing power in prayer or not, sending your good thoughts to people you have upset, offended or feel distant from can't do them any harm. The more you think positively about other people, the more you send out positive energy into the world. Should you connect with that person in real life, the firm foundation you have laid will make connecting with them so much more natural. And if you're never in contact with them again, you can rest easy knowing you are sending them positive and healing energy.

Take action

Think about someone in your life you are distanced from. That distance may be physical or because of a disagreement you had that has not been resolved. Maybe you have unfinished business between you. Choose who you want to focus your thoughts on and then make a conscious effort to send healing and positive energy to them.

You may struggle to do this at first, especially if you feel that this person has wronged you in some way. But the power of this exercise is to free you from the draining energy of anger, guilt and strong dislike, so that you put fewer negative emotions and thoughts out into the world and more positive ones instead. You can forgive someone without forgetting. It truly is worth giving this counterintuitive exercise a go every day for at least three weeks. You will be surprised by how it changes your attitude towards the person you are distanced from and may just find – as I have done whenever I practise this suggestion – that if you do encounter that person, they have inexplicably softened their attitude towards you or, at the very least, their hold over you has melted away. It's remarkable.

Sometimes kind intentions towards others can have as much healing power as kind actions.

Others – Way 48: Keep your word

These days, we hear a lot about fake news or alternative facts, which involve the spinning or manipulation of the truth to create a new reality. Sometimes that new reality can be so powerful it takes on a life of its own, even though it is divorced from the facts. We all colour our words with our own personal viewpoint, but one of the kindest things we can do is to uphold the truth.

Have you ever been put on hold by a company and then waited for an age listening to dreary music and the words, 'Your call is important to us', blasting in your ear? The chances are you have. Being misled by words like this doesn't make you feel good. Contrast this to calling a company and being connected within moments to a real person who both sorts out your query and wishes you a lovely day. It feels life-affirming to be treated with respect.

Simply being a person of your word and honest about your thoughts and feelings is an act of respect and kindness towards others that encourages them to be authentic with you, too. If you say you are going to do something or you promise something, keep your word. The essence of being kinder to others is being impeccable with your words[100] – always speaking with integrity, avoiding gossip and negativity and, most important of all, following through on your promises.

Take action

Vow that from now on you will only say what you truly mean and commit to doing what you are actually going to do. Of course, sometimes it may not be possible to follow through but, if this happens, apologise and explain why.

Carry this personal integrity into all your conversations and interactions. It's tempting to put on a brave face or to tell white lies

100 Ruiz, D.M. (1997) *The Four Agreements*. Amber-Allen Publishing.

to make others feel better, but this keeps conversations superficial. There is evidence[101] to suggest that the lower a person's self-esteem, the more likely they are to bend the truth, with men lying more to make themselves appear better and women lying more to make others feel better. Lying in any form is unkind.

Every time you are tempted to gossip, criticise or bend the truth, tap your heart with your hand as a physical reminder to always speak with integrity. Ask yourself the following three questions: Are my words truthful? Are they necessary? Are they kind? If you need to say something you feel is necessary but potentially hurtful, say it in a kind way or say nothing at all.

Sometimes being a person of integrity can prove costly, but success or popularity gained through deception or at the expense of others is empty and soul-destroying. There can be no greater tribute than to be described as a person of integrity, a man or woman of your word.

Others – Way 49: Spare the time

When we ask children what they want most from their parents, the answer doesn't tend to be presents or material things, it's to spend time together. And it's not just children who value time with loved ones, we all do. Time shared with loved ones is one of the most essential ingredients for a fulfilling life. It provides support and contributes greatly to our happiness and the happiness of those we love.

Although close relationships can also be a source of negativity – take action to surround yourself with supportive people if you are in toxic relationships – in general, social support from those closest to you with your best interests at heart is highly rewarding. Strong supportive relationships may also be good for both your

101 Feldman, R. (2002) 'Self-presentation and verbal deception: Do self-presenters lie more?' *Basic and Applied Social Psychology*, 24(2) 163–170.

mental and physical health, as there is evidence[102] to suggest that people who have them experience better health, reduced anxiety and depression and stronger immunity and longevity than those who do not.

The 2020 pandemic, which forced us all to contemplate our mortality as never before, may play a part in helping us reimagine our definition of a fulfilling life, so that we place less emphasis on material success and more on what and who really matter in our lives. Hopefully, we will choose to see success in terms of how much we have learned, how happy we feel, how positively our actions impact others, how compassionate we have been and what part we have played in making the world a kinder place. Time spent with dying people revealed to me that their thoughts are drawn towards moments of togetherness and the precious time spent with loved ones rather than promotion at work, expensive possessions, social media popularity or the latest technology. It's a cliché but, like many clichés, it's true: nobody on their deathbed says they wished they had spent more time at the office.

Take action

From now on, schedule regular time out with the people who matter most to you. So often in our busy lives, we take for granted those special people who are there for us no matter what. And sometimes, without meaning to, we can be darn right unkind to them, dismissive of their needs and not there for them when they need us.

It doesn't matter what you decide to do together during the time you schedule for the people who matter to you – sometimes just sitting in silence to watch the world go by in your garden or watching movies together can be a great bonding experience. And if you love animals, the same applies. Animals love us uncondi-

---

102 www.health.harvard.edu/newsletter_article/the-health-benefits-of-strong-relationships.

tionally and have such short lifespans. Spend as much time with them as you can.

Time, remember, is the kindest and most precious gift you can give anyone you care about. Ask someone who has ever lost a loved one. They would give anything to spend a few moments with them again. So, make time for the people in your life who count.

Others – Way 50: Be of service

Volunteering is a proactive and positive way to help make the world a kinder place. Offering your services for free or helping those who urgently need your spare funds, time or skills makes a real difference in shifting the world in the positive direction of compassion and connection. During the 2020 pandemic, volunteer response reached an all-time high, revealing the best of human nature. As the world resets, the hope is that we all continue to make volunteering or being of service to those less fortunate a constant theme.

This way to be kind encourages you to find ways to volunteer your services or help those who are less fortunate than you. Bear in mind that not only is being of service to others through volunteering your time without payment beneficial or potentially life-saving to those you are helping, it is also really good for you. Research[103] indicates that it truly is better for you to give than receive. Giving to others eases anxiety and depression and boosts mood and happiness. And being of service or volunteering on a regular basis can be especially beneficial if you are going through a hard time or feeling low yourself. Helping others less fortunate can help shift your perspective and give you a sense of meaning and purpose.

The volunteering world has moved with the times to fit any lifestyle or schedule. There are full-time, part-time, one-off, micro,

---

103 www.mentalhealth.org.uk/publications/doing-good-does-you-good.

skills-based, hands-on and remote opportunities, and many, many more ways to volunteer. While making a regular commitment is ideal, you do not have to donate huge amounts of time or even make a long-term commitment. So, there are no excuses!

Take action

Start in very simple ways: by buying a homeless person a hot drink, volunteering in a soup kitchen, joining a volunteer helpline, offering your skills or knowledge to charities or good causes online and in the real world, or simply by calling an elderly person to see if they need any help. It doesn't matter what you do, as long as you reach out to see if you can be of service to someone.

If you aren't sure how to get started with volunteering, you may wish to begin close to home. Do you have any vulnerable or elderly family members, neighbours or friends? How can you help or be of service to them? If you prefer to work remotely, there are plenty of chances to help charities or good causes online by either donating funds, mentoring or offering your skills and knowledge. Simply do an online search for 'volunteer opportunities' to explore what could match your skills and circumstances. You can also organise events, sell things or join in with sponsored activities to help raise funds for charities. You can mentor students. Nursing homes, hospitals and hospices always need volunteers. There is a whole new world of volunteering possibilities out there waiting for you to explore and, in the process, help make the world a more compassionate place.

Others – Way 51: Ask for and accept help

You may feel that it makes you appear weak or vulnerable to ask for help. In a survival-of-the-fittest culture, being self-sufficient seems the best and only approach, but what you may not realise is that asking for help isn't only about helping *you* or solving *your* problems. Just as being kind to others can make you feel better about yourself, so can helping you make others feel good about themselves and, as studies[104] show, improve their life satisfaction. So, in a roundabout way, you are spreading kindness every time you ask someone for advice or a helping hand.

If you've ever been stopped in the street by someone seeking directions, you have probably found yourself taking time to help them and apologising if you can't. You may not realise it, but the reason you made such an effort was that this stranger noticed you and felt safe to approach you. It's a compliment. They could have asked anyone, but they chose you and gave you an opportunity to be kind and feel better about yourself. I feel the same way whenever one of my readers messages me to ask for advice.

In spiritual terms, giving and receiving are interchangeable. If you find it hard to accept help, compliments or gifts from others, open yourself up to asking for help and receiving it with gratitude. Of course, you should try to solve issues or find things out for yourself first – and don't confuse asking for help with laziness – but, if you genuinely need a helping hand, you have nothing to lose and everything to gain from asking loved ones, friends or even strangers for help and advice.

Take action

From now on, change your thinking about asking others for help. Don't let pride or fear stop you spreading kindness. When you need a helping hand, admit your need and ask someone – and whether they offer that help or not, be sure to say thank you.

---

104 Andreoni, J. (1990) 'Impure altruism and donations to public goods: A theory of warm-glow giving?' *Economic Journal*, 100(401) 464–477.

You may feel that others are too busy, or they will think less of you or feel obliged in some way, but how other people feel about you and respond to your request is up to them, not you. If the person you ask is unable or unwilling to help you, they can simply say so. Don't take a negative response personally.

Remember that politely asking someone for help is not an imposition but a compliment. If you think of it this way, hopefully you will seek aid more often. The chances are, if someone can't help you directly, they will refer you to someone who can, because being asked for help has triggered their kindness 'muscle'. Either way, it's a real compliment to them that you singled them out as a wise or capable enough person to ask. You asking them for help makes them feel good. You are spreading kindness. It's incredibly life-affirming.

Others – Way 52: Mind your manners

Being kind makes you happier,[105] with one study assigning participants aged 18–60 to perform acts of kindness or no acts on a daily basis for ten days. Their life satisfaction was measured before and after the ten-day experiment. As expected, performing acts of kindness resulted in an increase in life satisfaction.

Nothing shows kindness more than being conscious of how your words and actions impact others. So, if you want to feel happier, one of the simplest ways is to be polite and show courtesy.

From an early age, most of us were taught to say 'please' and 'thank you'. As we get older, good manners can slide down our list of priorities, especially when life gets busy or stressful. But remembering to say 'thank you' or using that magic word 'please' isn't just the kindest way to live, it is also the most productive.

---

105 Buchanan, K. *et al.* (2010) 'Acts of kindness and acts of novelty affect life satisfaction.' *The Journal of Social Psychology*, 150(3) 235–237.

People respond better to you if they feel you respect them enough to be polite and courteous.

Showing consideration to others is the gentle glue that keeps society[106] together. If people don't value politeness and courtesy, rudeness and selfishness take hold. That's why we spend so much time trying to teach children the importance of manners in all their interactions, and why schools, companies and organisations have rules of conduct. Respecting those rules doesn't just bring order and harmony, it also says a great deal about you. It shows that you are the kind of person who considers others and that's the kind of person every society needs.

Good manners are worth the time and effort because they can improve all areas of your life. It's tempting to take loved ones and friends for granted and think that good manners don't matter as much at home, but they truly do. If you are a parent, setting a good example motivates your children to follow. At work, politeness is a sign of respect for your colleagues that they likely mirror back to you. Courtesy towards friends encourages them to want you in their life, and kindness towards strangers inspires everyone to make the world a kinder place.

Take action

The golden rule is to treat others as you'd like them to treat you. Start by using the words 'please' and 'thank you' more often and try to eliminate swear words. If you want help or ask for something, say 'please'. If others send you gifts, offer you compliments or help, accept them gratefully and say 'thank you' or send messages or notes of gratitude, knowing that you are helping them experience the joy of giving. If someone does

---

106 Spencer-Oatey, H. & Kádár, D. (2016) 'The basis of (im)politeness evaluations: Culture, the moral order and the East-West debate.' *East Asian Pragmatics*, 1, 75–108.

well, compliment them. If someone is walking behind you, hold the door open for them. Politeness and courtesy require being mindful of others.

Practise and prioritise good manners and courtesy so that they become second nature to you. This can boost your self-confidence because, wherever you go and whatever you do, you know you will automatically say or do the right, and therefore kind, thing.

Others – Way 53: Show a little patience

There's no saying it any other way. The modern world can be an extremely frustrating place. Queues can be long. Waiting times may last an age. Technology tends to break down. People don't do what they promise. There's often rejection or setbacks. How to cope?

It's natural to try to force things to run smoothly, to make other people fall into line, and to react with frustration and impatience. We live in a fast world and expect instant results. But the kindest thing to do for both yourself and others when things aren't going to plan – which, let's face it, happens often – is to show patience.

Often associated with being passive, unimaginative, weak or resigned, patience is anything but. Rather it is being independent, strong-willed and compassionate. It is understanding that life isn't perfect and wasn't meant to be, and that human beings are fallible. It is also being intuitive and knowing when to react and when to put things on hold. There are some things in life you can control and some you can't, and being patient is one you can.

Impatience not only raises stress levels and hurts your heart and your health,[107] it invariably upsets, offends and unsettles others, puts them on the defensive and damages relationships. So, this

---

107 www.livescience.com/25085-impatience-may-hurt-heart.html.

way to be kinder to others encourages you to choose patience whenever you feel the tension rising. Even if you are hot-headed, you can learn patience as a skill, according to research[108] which encouraged participants to take part in a training programme to increase their patient traits, and this training led to increased patience and decreased depression. Think of patience as a choice you make to wait until the time is right to act.

Take action

Patience is a skill that, once mastered, can serve you for a life-time. When you practise it daily you are being kinder to others as well as to yourself. Next time you feel a wave of frustration when you're waiting in a long queue, things are stuck or delayed or not going to plan, or people are letting you down, resist the urge to say or do anything. Close your eyes, take a long, deep breath and silently tell yourself that you are going to enjoy the pause.

You may simply wish to enjoy the opportunity to daydream, or spend the time completing another task. You can also choose to flex your empathy 'muscle' by identifying with and saying something encouraging to the person causing the delay or frustration, or you can decide to joke or make light of the situation. Every time you choose patience – and the inner peace that comes with it – you will notice how much more in control you feel and how much others appreciate or admire your choice.

A little patience in all your dealings with others can go a long way to making the world a kinder place. From now on, regard those frustrating situations in everyday life as opportunities to choose patience and all the life-affirming benefits associated with it.

---

108 Schnitker, K. *et al.* (2012) 'An examination of patience and well-being.' *The Journal of Positive Psychology*, 7(4) 263–280.

Others – Way 54: Aim higher

Have you ever been with a group of people when the conversation turns towards someone else? You are likely to be drawn in and give your own opinion, and there is nothing wrong with that. Human beings are social creatures, and research[109] shows that discussing what others are doing with their lives is a great way to bond and share useful information. But what do you do when you hear negative things about the person being discussed or private details you know they don't want shared? Your instinct is likely to be to join in the gossip because the desire to be liked and included in a group often overrides the wish to do the kind thing. But how do you feel afterwards?

If you are like most gentle people, you probably feel a little compromised or tarnished. A part of you may also wonder if the people in the group could easily turn on you in the same way. Michelle Obama, the former US First Lady, once said, 'When they go low, we go higher', and her words are an anthem for a kinder world. Don't be tempted to follow the herd – they might just lead you off the cliff because negative gossip simply pumps unkindness into the world. Instead, choose to aim higher and avoid negativity.

Take action

In Way 31 to be kinder online, an important rule was that if you wouldn't say something to someone's face, you shouldn't say it online either. The same applies when you are talking about people with others. If you hear something negative about someone and they are not there to defend themselves, point this out and step out of the conversation. This may alienate you from the group, but you need to consider why you would want to be part of a group or conversation that aims so low. Your decision not

---

109 https://time.com/5680457/why-do-people-gossip.

to engage may have a positive impact on others and encourage them to do the same. That old cliché is once again very true: 'If you have nothing nice to say, say nothing at all.'

And it's not just when you are talking about others that you should rise above negativity. There is research[110] to suggest that people can 'catch' or pick up on the feelings of others. So, if you are feeling low, irritable or angry, don't spread that feeling – it's not kind or helpful. It's important to resist the urge to vent your frustration on others. Give yourself some time out. Punch a cushion. Go for a run or a brisk walk. Step away from interactions with others and see the bigger picture. If you can do this, not only will you be part of the kindness revolution, you will also feel good about yourself.

Note: Should you ever feel powerless to manage negative thoughts, seek advice from your doctor.

Others – Way 55: Let them off the hook

When dealing with other people, perhaps the wisest advice to remember is that you never know what someone else is going through. Sometimes people can appear irritable and unreasonable or lash out at you for no apparent reason, but for all you know they could have had some bad news or be in pain. In an ideal world, we should never take out our frustrations on others but, being far from perfect, we do. So, it makes sense to give others a break or the benefit of the doubt whenever possible (of course, you should never tolerate abuse of any kind).

---

110 Kimura, M. *et al.* (2008) 'The study of emotional contagion from the perspective of interpersonal relationships.' *Social Behavior and Personality: An International Journal*, 36(1) 27–42.

Letting people off the hook is also tied up with another important thing you can do to be kinder to others and that is release them from the expectations of how you feel they should behave or be. Studies[111] suggest that one of the major reasons for relationship breakdown is wanting others to be the person we think they should be. It's falling in love with or liking a person because of their potential, rather than who they are. If you don't love or like the person for who they are right now – warts and all – then the relationship isn't going to work. When people show you who they are, believe them. You can't change others – only they can do that.

Take action

The next time you are tempted to retaliate when someone is unreasonable or lashes out, take a step back. Think of them as a human being with a lot going on in their life. Choose to think the best of them and let it go. Of course, if they repeat the behaviour, call it out and put a stop to it. But if it is a one-off or it happens now and again, give them the benefit of the doubt.

Carry this relaxed attitude with you in your interactions with everyone, including strangers. For example, if someone bumps into you accidently, don't yell at them and preach that they should be paying more attention. Recall all the times you have been preoccupied and have not paid attention to what is going on around you. Why not say, 'That's okay. It happens to us all', and give them a big smile. Nine times out of ten that is more likely to encourage them to be more careful in future than if you shouted at them. Kindness is a powerful teacher, as the person will already know they are in the wrong and be grateful to you for not making them feel worse.

---

111 Frost, D.M *et al.* (2013) 'Closeness discrepancies in romantic relationships: Implications for relational well-being, stability, and mental health.' *Personality and Social Psychology Bulletin*, 39(4) 456–469.

Moving forward, in your interactions see others not as the people you want them to be but as who they are right now. See and love them as fellow human beings – learning and growing and simply doing the best they can, just as you are.

Others – Way 56: Just say 'no'

Kind people like you probably say the word 'yes' a lot. People are drawn to your positivity and it feels good helping them. This way to be kind is not going to ask you to stop saying yes when others reach out for your help, as that would be the same as asking you to stop being kind. After all, the world needs more, not fewer, kind people like you, who truly care about the wellbeing of others. This way is going to ask you to say 'no' as many times as you say 'yes'.

Being busy is a badge of honour these days. Most of us have never-ending 'to-do' lists of things we need to get done. The problem is, the busier you are, the less opportunity you have to be kind because you are overcommitted and preoccupied. It is important to focus on what really matters and that starts with the ability to devote your energy to the people and things that matter to you most. Unbelievably, many of us spend the least amount of our time with the people we love the most! So, this way to be kind encourages you to say 'no' to any commitments or demands that are not essential, are unnecessarily distracting or drain your energy. Research[112] shows that saying 'no' more often frees up your energy to be kinder to others and yourself.

Take action

It may not always feel that way, but it is sometimes kinder to others to say 'no' rather than 'yes'. If someone is taking advan-

---

112 https://greatergood.berkeley.edu/images/uploads/Weinstein-
    MindfulnessStress.pdf.

tage, asking you to do things they could do themselves, say 'no'. If you are doing all the work and others are coasting, say 'no'. If someone makes an unreasonable request, politely say 'no'. By encouraging people to do things for themselves, you are being kind to both them and yourself, as you are prioritising who and what matter to you and devoting your energy to them.

Many of us these days have become accomplished multi-taskers. We are talking to someone but have our eye on our phone and our thoughts on what to buy for dinner. Not only does this make the person feel unimportant, it makes us feel unfulfilled and unhappy, too. There is a reason why the mindfulness movement has dominated in recent years, with psychologists and health gurus promoting it everywhere. It simply encourages us to say 'no' to the distractions that take us away from the present and to the demands of everyday life. Mindfulness is choosing to be in the moment and giving the task in hand or the person you are connecting with your complete and undivided attention. Try switching your phone to silent, then consciously look people in the face and focus solely on your interaction with them. By giving others all your attention, you are showing love, kindness and respect for them, yourself and your life. So, say 'no' to distractions and to what is not necessary or essential and focus on those who matter most to you.

Others – Way 57: Donate with care

The success of sites like eBay, where anyone can sell their personal items to the highest bidder, clearly demonstrates that one person's junk is someone else's treasure. So, whenever you declutter your home or office or clear out your wardrobe, consider who might benefit from your unwanted things before you throw them in a skip or consign them to the dump.

You may think the next best thing is to donate your pre-loved clothes, books, electronics and other items to a charity or good cause but, although this can be helpful, it is not always the kindest thing to do. Do you simply want to get rid of 'stuff' or truly help your community? If you want to help, consider the perspective of the charity. Perhaps they are already inundated with unwanted items by well-meaning people. If so, it would be better to find ways to give them away or sell those items yourself and then give the organisation the proceeds instead. You can personally gift your unwanted items to people and places that you know would be very grateful for them – for example, magazines and toys to dentists and hospitals for their waiting rooms and books to school and prison libraries.

And don't stop at material or financial donations, but also consider those of a personal nature. You can use your body to save lives. Indeed, research[113] shows that there may be a connection between life satisfaction and blood donation, and that the incidence of depression[114] is consistently low in organ donors. Perhaps this is because donating to others – literally giving up a part of yourself or letting go of something only you can give – in this altruistic way makes people feel good about themselves.

Take action

Most of us have far too much 'stuff'. So, commit to regular clear-outs and ensure that you give what you no longer need to someone who will value or use it, or sell it and donate the proceeds to charity.

If you are healthy, why not become a regular blood donor? You may never know whether your blood is used for research or for saving a life, but either way you are giving away something

---

113 Alfieri, S. *et al.* (2017) '"Just" blood donors? A study on the multi-affiliations of blood donors.' *Transfusion and Apheresis Science*, 56(4) 578–584. doi: 10.1016/j.transci.2017.07.019.

114 https://onlinelibrary.wiley.com/doi/abs/10.1111/ctr.13838.

priceless for your fellow human beings. You can also donate your hair if you decide to have it cut off. And if you wish to offer even more, get in touch with your doctor to discuss possible donations ranging from plasma or bone marrow to sperm or eggs to stem cells.

One of the kindest things you can ever do should you die, is to give medical professionals the opportunity to harvest your organs to give someone else a chance of life. This is a deeply personal choice and whatever decision you make will be right for you, but it is something that all of us should at the very least consider.

Others – Way 58: Reach out to those in crisis

This way to be kind offers you more counterintuitive advice, but it does so for a good reason. Many of us limit our potential for spreading kindness because we are more concerned about doing the 'right' thing than doing the kind thing. This deliberation and fear of messing up typically paralyses us and stops us doing anything at all.

A classic example is when someone has lost a loved one. Our natural instinct is to offer the bereaved person a shoulder to cry on, to talk to them about the person they have lost or to offer help. But all too often we avoid them for fear of saying the 'wrong' thing or upsetting them further. Although this reluctance comes from the right place, being left alone is the last thing most grieving people want.

Over the years I've been writing spiritual books, a running theme – and one backed up by research[115] – has been the loneliness of bereavement. One widow wrote to me that after her partner's funeral her friends and family vanished. She said this made her

---

115 van Baarsen, B. *et al.* (2002) 'Theories on coping with loss: The impact of social support and self-esteem on adjustment to emotional and social loneliness following a partner's death in later life.' *The Journals of Gerontology: Series B*, 57(1) S33–S42.

grief even harder to bear. And when people did find the courage to talk to her, nobody mentioned her loss or her departed partner, whom she urgently did want to talk about, to honour his memory and keep alive their relationship in her heart. She didn't want to move on and forget him because he was still a part of her.

This is true for every bereaved person and whenever I explain to them that the avoidant behaviour of others is not intentional, their advice is always the same: 'I won't be offended. Just talk to me about the person I have lost. Say their name.'

Take action

If you know someone who has lost a loved one, or who is having any kind of extreme life crisis, such as being diagnosed with a terminal illness, going through a relationship break-up or divorce or being made redundant, don't avoid them for fear of doing the wrong thing. The only wrong thing you can do is avoid someone who needs help. They require others' support urgently in their time of need, even if they don't request or articulate it. And if there is nothing you can do for them practically, or they tell you that they need time alone, simply let them know you are there for them if they ever want help or someone to listen – your willingness will mean the world to them.

If you feel anxious or don't know how to start a conversation with someone going through trauma, you need to accept that the situation isn't going to be comfortable and that is okay because life isn't always comfortable. Remember to make the conversation about them, not you, and don't be afraid of being together with that person in silence. Your interaction with them lets them know you care. When someone has died, you can ask them about their deceased loved one as they don't want to forget or move on. If someone has gone through a relationship break-up, they also will feel they have lost a part of themselves. Talking things through can really help them rediscover their identity and not feel so alone. If someone has lost a job or suffered financial loss, let them vent but then encourage them to move forward and be proactive in finding solutions. And if someone has suddenly received bad news, perhaps a health crisis, be aware their whole life may feel blown apart. Again, listen and let them know you are there for them and how much they mean to you.

Even if your offer to be there or help is pushed away, know that you are doing the right and kind thing by reaching out – the human thing. Carry forward this advice into other situations when you aren't sure if your kindness is the 'right' thing to do. Always listen to your heart – it knows what is best to do.

Others – Way 59: Treat strangers well

In ancient times, showing kindness only to family and people you knew and treating strangers with extreme caution was justified. Stranger danger was real and a potential threat to safety and even survival. But the world has moved on and the majority of us leave home and the communities we were born into to build our lives elsewhere. We travel more, and community doesn't mean as much. Although this can feel liberating, it can also lead to feelings of isolation and loneliness. Indeed, recent surveys[116] have found that loneliness has become a modern disease even though we are better connected online than ever before.

That's why always treating people you don't know and may never see again with kindness is incredibly important, because you don't know how your kind words or actions may impact that person's life. You may never know or hear back but acts of kindness towards strangers – even just a smile, a kind word or holding open

---

116 www.bbc.co.uk/programmes/articles/2yzhfv4DvqVp5nZyxBD8G23/who-feels-lonely-the-results-of-the-world-s-largest-loneliness-study.

a door for them – change the world for the better, one random act of kindness at a time.

Be aware of an unconscious tendency to stick with those who are similar to you or who share your culture or beliefs. This urge to merge with what is similar to us in others can feel validating because when we surround ourselves with people who are like us or look like us, we feel accepted, like we belong. In times past, this was for survival reasons as the tribe protected its own. But today the urge to merge with what is similar can become toxic. It creates a 'them and us' mentality and focuses on difference rather than similarity between human beings. Centuries of unjust focus on difference rather than similarity erupted in 2020 with the protests about racism. The world was long overdue for a racial reset and if you take anything from this book, I hope it is to remind you that kindness can help reshape the world because it does not discriminate. Kindness is not just for people you love or care about or who agree with you or resonate with you in some way. Kindness is for everyone you encounter in your life.

Take action

Being kind to strangers doesn't have to involve much time and effort. Of course, you can do some more lengthy things, for example undertaking a sponsored run for someone you've heard needs life-saving treatment or manning the volunteer phone lines in a crisis centre – but there are easier ways to make kindness towards strangers a way of life. Begin by always wishing people well, regardless of who they are or what they look like. *Focus on shared humanity.* We all have basic human needs. We all need to eat, drink and get a good night's sleep and we all need a roof over our heads. We all go through hard times. We all have beating hearts. We all bleed, and we all need help and a kind word from time to time.

So, as you go about your day, think about how you would like to be treated. Smile and say hello, if the opportunity arises. If you are reserved and this doesn't come naturally to you, don't force it. Find other ways to be kind, such as holding the lift door open for someone or letting someone go in front of you in a queue; you could offer change if you see someone struggling to find the right amount, or you could simply ask someone who is serving you in some way, how they are.

Treat strangers as you would wish to be treated and you can't go wrong. If you find your friendliness sometimes encounters suspicion, don't let that deter you. The majority of people will respond to your smile by smiling back, but if they don't, wish them well silently and understand that some people have reasons for feeling anxious. Don't forget to be kind to younger people, too. Contrary to popular belief, loneliness is not just for the elderly. Young adults are feeling lonelier than ever and may well appreciate a smile from a stranger more than anyone else.

Others – Way 60: Stay open

There are over seven billion people on this planet and although you are inevitably drawn to people going through similar life experiences and stages as you, and who share or understand your viewpoint, you also encounter far more who are in a different life stage or who disagree with you or come with a radically different perspective. The basis of friendship is shared experience and belief. For example, when you are at school or college, you are likely to bond with people who take the same subjects as you. People always promise to keep in touch when they leave school or graduate, but typically they gradually drift apart as their lives and careers progress. It's simply the journey of life. As you evolve, the people you are drawn to suit the different ages and stages of your life.

There is such a thing as a friend for life, but to maintain life-long friendships both people need to accept and understand the other's changing interests and circumstances. That's why this way to be kind is all about avoiding judgement, letting other people be who they need to be and, most importantly, keeping an open mind. In the five-factor model of human personality that psychologists use,[117] openness is a key element that makes up human experience, and people who are open-minded tend to be more curious, optimistic, empathic and kind.

Tunnel vision and lack of understanding and respect for difference are major causes of conflict and tension, not just in friendships and close relationships but in the world in general. Start to educate yourself about cultures and beliefs different from your own. Open your mind. Don't rush to judge. The 2020 race riots happened for a reason, as many of us simply haven't considered and respected viewpoints different from our own. Be part of the trend for inclusion rather than exclusion. Show acceptance and understanding towards everyone, and also be curious and willing to learn. See if you can understand where people who are different from you are coming from – you might just learn something to shift your perspective. Remember, listening and understanding is not the same as agreeing. It is relating to your fellow human beings with love.

Take action

Just because somebody believes something you don't or is going through an experience you can't relate to, or looks very different from you, it doesn't make it wrong.

The next time you find yourself unable to agree with a loved one or a friend or encounter someone whose way of life is radically

---

117 Power, R.A. *et al.* (2015) 'Heritability estimates of the Big Five personality traits based on common genetic variants.' *Translational Psychiatry*, 5(7) e604.

different from your own, don't criticise or judge. Let them be or do what they feel they need to. (Of course, if you feel someone is in danger or putting themselves in harm's way, alert friends and family and, if need be, your local doctor or police.) Always try to understand different perspectives. Open your mind and learn what you can, and, if you still disagree, politely agree to disagree. The world would be a very dull place if we were all the same. Variety is the spice of life.

Be tolerant also when dealing with people in different age groups from yours. Do you get impatient when you are behind someone elderly on the stairs? That person could be you one day. Do you get irritated by the exuberance of teenagers or the screams of young children in a playground? Remember, you were young once, too.

If your need to judge and criticise or see others as somehow inferior, separate or different, consider this basic psychological truth: what you dislike or condemn in others may be something you fear or are not acknowledging within yourself.

Others – Way 61: Make connections

There's a lot of truth in the well-known phrase, 'It's not *what* you know, but *who* you know.' Many of my lucky breaks have resulted because someone I knew or worked with before put in a good word for me or recommended me. Although people like to feel they are making their own decisions, it's human nature to be influenced by the opinions of others, especially those they know and trust.

If you've ever been asked to be someone's referee or to endorse them, it gives you a confidence shot. Someone considers you significant enough for your opinion to matter and to be trusted. If you are asked to be a referee, the kindest thing is to be honest. Of course, you want the person to get the job or the project and you do all you can to present them in the best possible light. But you also need to ensure that they are the right person for the job. You won't be doing them or your reputation any favours by bending the truth or omitting information. This way to be kind isn't about responding to people who ask you to recommend or endorse them, it's about sharing your network to help connect people you think could work well together or benefit from being introduced.

Networking is an important part of success. Online professional platforms like LinkedIn prove this, but research[118] shows that, for most of us, cold networking is a painful experience. People much prefer to be introduced to someone new, whether in person or virtually, by someone they already know.

Over the years, I have built up amazing connections with editors and publishers, practitioners, scientists, psychologists, experts and healers. One of the most rewarding things about my work is that I am now in a position to make connections if I can. Someone may get in touch saying they wish they knew how to write a proposal or asking which publisher might be suitable or which expert might be able to advise them and, if I can, I try to make recommendations. It's very satisfying to see them thrive from the connection made.

Take action

If you know and work with skilled individuals, it's tempting to try to keep them all to yourself, but this is done from a position of fear. Success does not have a limit on it – it grows the more it is shared.

If you hear of someone who needs something and you know just the person to provide it, don't keep your knowledge to yourself. Suggest that person or, better still, put them in touch. Sure, you

---

118 Ingram, P. (2007) 'Do people mix at mixers? Structure, homophily, and the "life of the party".' *Administrative Science Quarterly, Cornell School of Business*, 52(4) 558–585.

might be left out as they move forward but, if you have played a part in helping them progress, you have helped to make the world kinder.

Others – Way 62: See the person behind the job

Whenever you interact with a uniformed official of any kind, be it a police officer or a parking attendant, or someone such as a salesperson, receptionist or valet, respect their profession but try not to judge them by their job title or the uniform they are wearing. It's human nature to rely on stereotypes[119] based on what we initially perceive about them. But all accountants are not boring, and all parking attendants are not 'jobsworths', and nor does every person wearing a hoodie have criminal intent. Every person is a unique individual and, although their choice of career may say something about them, it does not say it all. Try to think of every person – whether you admire their career choice or not – as someone simply doing their best, just as you are trying to do your best too.

And as well as not judging, make a point of seeing the human being behind the job and treat everyone with equal kindness and respect. You can tell a great deal about a person from the way they treat people they don't think really matter. If you are with someone who is going out of their way to make you feel valued but then notice them yelling at a waiter or ignoring the doorman holding the door open for them, that's a relationship red flag.

Take action

If you have an instinctive bias against people who do a specific job, the first step is to become aware of it. The chances are you've

119 Hinton, P. (2017) 'Implicit stereotypes and the predictive brain: Cognition and culture in "biased" person perception.' *Palgrave Communications* 3, 17086. https://doi.org/10.1057/palcomms.2017.86.

picked up this bias from stereotypes presented in books and films or from other people in your life who influenced your perception. Once you are aware of your bias, make a conscious effort to minimise it. If you do get a parking ticket, don't yell at the parking officer as it's not their fault. They are just doing their job. If you get irritated by people in the street constantly asking you to do a survey, why not give them a few moments of your time, if you aren't truly in a rush? Help them do their job and get the numbers and information they need. If you encounter someone pedantic who lets rules and regulations override common sense, again try to understand where they are coming from.

Carry forward this respect for who people are behind what they do into all areas of your life. It's one of the kindest and most healing things you can do, both for the people you know and for strangers. Feeling respected and valued is a basic human need. So, thank the receptionist, tip the waiter, smile at the door attendant and the rest-room attendant. If you want to be kinder to others, make everyone you encounter or interact with, whether they are a newspaper seller, a road sweeper, a colleague or a VIP, feel noticed and valued.

Others – Way 63: Shine your light

Many of us don't fear failure, what we really fear is succeeding, shining and standing out. We fear the reactions or rejections of others. Former US presidential candidate, Marianne Williamson,[120] highlighted this so perfectly when she said, 'There is nothing "enlightened" about shrinking so that other people won't feel insecure around you. We are all meant to shine…'

This way to be kind asks you to step into your own power and never be afraid to shine brightly as is your birthright. It also sets

---

120 Williamson, M. (2015) *A Return to Love*. Harper Thorson (reissue), p.165.

an inspiring example for others to follow. You would be forgiven for thinking that this way to be kind belongs in a previous section – how to be kinder to yourself – but I placed it here because, whether you realise it or not, finding within yourself the courage to shine inspires others to look within themselves and discover what they need for their own happiness and fulfilment. In this way, you become a positive role model – someone aspirational, motivating them to raise the bar and step into their own power.

Even if the reaction your inner joy triggers in others is envy, it's a powerful way to show people what they need in their lives. And if your joy and success do cost you friends, that's a positive thing too, because such people were never friends in the first place. True friends want the best for the people they care about.

Take action

Memorise these immortal lines by Williamson: 'Our deepest fear is not that we are inadequate. Our deepest fear is that we are powerful beyond measure. It is our light, not our darkness that most frightens us.' Every time you are tempted to hide, make excuses or diminish yourself, say these words out loud. Remind yourself that hiding your light serves neither you nor others.

Whenever you have good news, don't keep it to yourself. Share it. Of course, you need to be sensitive and avoid showboating. If someone is going through a hard time, don't brag about your happiness. But don't hide it completely either, because doing that isn't honest or respectful to the other person. Relationships need honesty to flourish.

Start thinking of yourself as a kindness role model or mentor. If you are a parent, remember that children are copycats. The more often they see you content and treating yourself and others with kindness, the more they will think of that as a natural state of being. At work, be a model of contentment for your colleagues. Smile and treat everyone with respect. Do kind things to set the tone. Remember people's names and birthdays, hold doors open, make the tea or coffee unprompted, and so on. Showcase not just being kind, but the joy of being kind. In all areas of your life encourage others – be someone who sees the good rather than the bad, who doesn't find fault but spots the shining potential of everyone lucky enough to cross their path.

Others – Way 64: Receive with thanks

Being kinder to others has been shown[121] to make people feel happier. So, carry on thinking of ways to be kinder to the other people in your life as it's going to make you feel great. But what about when you find yourself on the receiving end of people's kindness? Should you accept? One hundred per cent, yes! You should never hesitate to accept with sincere gratitude any kindness or help others offer you with the best intentions.

If you feel embarrassed whenever someone goes out of their way to remember or thank you, or to help you, you are by no means alone. Have you ever refused to accept a gift because you have felt that the other person couldn't afford it or you are not worthy of receiving it? Or perhaps you have gone to lunch with a friend and, when they offered to pay, had a mini 'argument' because you felt you should pay? Even if that hasn't happened to you, you have probably witnessed it, as it can be quite comical when both parties refuse to accept the kindness offered to them.

This way to be kinder to others encourages you to get over yourself and to understand that it's not weak or greedy to accept

---

121 https://greatergood.berkeley.edu/article/item/kindness_makes_you_happy_and_happiness_makes_you_kind.

help offered with good intentions. Quite the opposite. Accepting it is being both kind to yourself – by acknowledging you are worth it – and, perhaps more surprisingly, kind to the other person too because, by letting them help you, you are allowing them to experience the gratifying 'helper's high' (see Chapter 1).

Take action

Next time, and from now on going forward, when someone pays you compliments or offers you a gift or unexpected help, don't throw it back in their face by getting embarrassed or refusing to accept, but flash them a smile and accept with gratitude. Say 'thank you' out loud and mean it. If they don't give you the gift in person, make sure that you send them a note or a text to thank them. Thank you notes may seem old-fashioned in the digital age, and sometimes you may find yourself thanking people for gifts you don't really want – did your great aunt really have to send you more purple socks you won't wear? – but that's no excuse. Focus not on the gift itself – you can always recycle that or find a good use for it – but concentrate on the fact that someone thought kindly of you.

And while we are on the subject of gratitude, why not make 'thank you' your favourite phrase from now on, not just for people but also the universe in gratitude for all the free but priceless gifts it sends you every day, such as sunshine, beautiful flowers or the birds singing? The more you open yourself up to receiving from others, and cultivate an attitude of gratitude[122], the more likely you are to attract good things into your life.

---

122 Emmons, R. (2008) *Thanks: How Practising Gratitude Can Make You Happier.* Mariner.

Others – Way 65: Recommend a good book

Previously you learned that research[123] has shown being a regular reader, particularly of fiction, might make you a nicer person. In Kingston University's study, after being questioned about their preferences for books, TV and theatre, the participants were tested on their social skills, including how much they considered other people's feelings and whether they helped others. The study discovered that readers were most likely to act in kinder ways than those who preferred going to the theatre or watching TV. People who preferred TV came across as less kind and empathetic. As well as being kinder, fiction readers were more open-minded and willing to tolerate and respect perspectives different from their own. And if that isn't enough to make you open up a novel, book readers may also make better lovers, as surveys[124] conducted on dating sites show that people with thoughtful reading lists or book choices get a better response!

So, one way to become kinder to others is to read a gripping work of fiction, but another great way is to recommend a book.

Take action

If you have read a book and it spoke to you or inspired you, don't keep it to yourself, recommend it to others so they can feel the beneficial impact too. You can do this impersonally by leaving helpful reviews saying why the book is a must-read on book-reviewing sites like Goodreads, but you can also personally recommend it to people you know. Sometimes books can be incredibly healing, especially if the book resonates with the person

---

123 Kingston University. 'Reading may make us kinder, student's research into fiction habits and personality types reveals.' *ScienceDaily*, 23 May 2017.

124 www.independent.co.uk/life-style/love-sex/book-readers-best-lovers-bilbiophiles-hunger-games-sex-attractive-richard-branson-men-women-a7708091.html.

you are suggesting reads it, because they may have experienced situations it describes.

Fiction seems to have the most positive impact on our wellbeing, and you are really doing someone a favour if you recommend a title that you have enjoyed, because it can be hard to know where to start if you want a good book. These days, with bookshops and libraries closing fast, physically browsing the bookshelves may become a thing of the past. So, a personal recommendation from a friend or someone you know can be really helpful.

However, non-fiction books can be just as therapeutic as fiction, so don't feel you have to stick with fiction in your recommendations. Sometimes non-fiction books, especially those on personal growth and development, can be life-changing. There is a book out there to help with any personal challenge, and the chances are that if it helped you, it could help others too. Indeed, recommending a self-help title when someone is going through a hard time can be a simple and kind way to support them.

It's probably not a good idea to buy someone a book unless you know them well, because they may feel obliged rather than excited to read it. People like to make their own choices, so bear that in mind when recommending books to them. Having said that, there is something very lovely and thoughtful in buying or receiving a book when you know someone has put a lot of thought into selecting or recommending it for you.

Others – Way 66: Hug with power

The emergence of social distancing in 2020 to stem the pandemic significantly reduced our ability to reach out and touch both our loved ones and anyone in our life. It's surely no coincidence that the first places to see large spikes were Italy and Spain, in cultures known for their relaxed physical intimacy, where hugging and kissing as greetings are commonplace.

One of the most heart-breaking consequences of the pandemic was that people died alone because loved ones were not allowed to be by their side, as they would have been previously. Social distancing meant that grandparents stayed in their cars to wave to their grandchildren, and families, loved ones and friends from separate households were kept apart. Phone and video calls were lifesavers, but they simply couldn't replace contact in person.

Physical contact with loved ones, friends and all the people we encounter in our lives is something we have taken for granted, despite there being science[125] to show that hugs have happiness- and immunity-boosting power. They can ease stress, aches and pains and promote heart health.[126] And as the world moves forward, we will hopefully never forget again what a priceless way to be kind giving others a hug is.

Take action

Whenever it's safe and acceptable to do so, reach out and hug your loved ones and friends much more. Be aware that everyone has different levels of comfort with physical intimacy, and adjust accordingly. If hugging makes someone uncomfortable, they won't get the benefits, so respect their need for distance.

It seems that receiving many hugs is better than not receiving enough, with four a day perhaps the minimum to feel a benefit. But what about hugging others? Many people these days are touch-deprived or work virtually, with reduced social interaction. The pandemic has, for good reason, forced us to hug or touch each other less than ever before, so if you get an opportunity to

125 Inagaki, T.K. *et al.* (2012) 'Neural correlates of giving support to a loved one.' *Pychosomatic Medicine*, 74(1) 3–7.

126 Grewen, K.M. *et al.* (2003) 'Warm partner contact is related to lower cardiovascular reactivity.' *Behavioral Medicine*, 29(3) 123–130.

give or receive a hug these days, and you trust the other person, don't miss it.

The best way to introduce more hugging into your life is to start with those closest to you – your family and friends. You may want to stop there, which is fine, because even hugging those closest to you more often is one of the kindest and most beneficial things you can do for them. If you do feel confident enough to hug others outside your inner circle, perhaps build up to it by first shaking their hand or patting them on the shoulder. Never invade someone's space uninvited, as they may feel violated. Heartfelt hugs are a powerful feel-good gift you can give someone, but only hug when it's safe and, above all, welcome.

Others – Way 67: Try movie therapy

Have you ever watched a film, a TV show or a YouTube video and been bursting to share it because it made you laugh or cry or it contained some fascinating new insights, perspectives or creative talking points for discussion? There's a reason for this. Movies contain symbols and themes that generate empathy and increase communication skills.

You've already seen how beneficial reading more fiction can be for boosting empathy, kindness and new perspectives, and movie therapy works along the same lines. The therapist suggests a film to their client that explores issues relevant to them. They are told to watch it and then they discuss their reactions in a mindful way and explore connections in their own life. Movie therapy is actually a term coined in the 1990s[127] by psychotherapists.

This fun way to be kind encourages you to recommend movies, TV shows or videos that you feel will inspire family, friends, loved ones and colleagues and perhaps also even open their eyes to new

127 Berg-Cross, L. *et al.* (1990) 'Cinematherapy: Theory and application.' *Psychotherapy in Private Practice*, 8, 135–156.

solutions. Films are widely available and accessible these days, and as watching them is such a fun experience, few people are going to object to your recommendations.

Take action

Start by recommending movies that have simply inspired you. You can't go wrong with life-affirming films like *It's a Wonderful Life*, *The Wizard of Oz*, *The Greatest Showman* or *Mamma Mia*. The chances are people will already have seen them but, if they haven't, what a gift you are giving them by encouraging them to perhaps feel as uplifted as you did after viewing them.

If you want to be more specific, you can start recommending movies tailored to help a person's situation. For example, if a friend is feeling sad, you can recommend your favourite comedy, though be aware that humour is subjective. If friends are feeling down, I always recommend the Disney movie *Inside Out* to help them come to terms with feelings of sadness. When someone is feeling as if they don't fit in, I always recommend both *Frozen* movies, and when someone is finding it hard to move forward with their life following a bereavement, I suggest the movie *Up* as it is a powerful study in integrating loss. You may have noticed that my movie recommendations are animated ones. There is a reason for that. When dealing with sensitive or emotional subjects, sometimes an animation is easier and gentler to process than real actors playing the part.

If you are finding it hard to broach a sensitive subject with someone, such as emotional abuse or addiction, discussing movies with these themes might get a positive conversation started. Indeed, conversations about fictional film characters are a great way to initiate conversations and connect better with others. Studies[128]

---

128 www.telegraph.co.uk/news/health/3330249/Movie-therapy-Do-you-believe-in-the-healing-power-of-film.html

have even shown that people who watch movies regularly together, and discuss them, communicate better and feel more positively about each other.

Others – Way 68: Let in fun

Life can get so intense and serious at times. And for good reason. Never was this more apparent than when the Coronavirus pandemic struck in 2020 and the world experienced its deadly impact. Every single day, news reports of lives lost and businesses closing bombarded our screens and our minds. There was despair and chaos all around. And even without a pandemic, our lives can still often be filled with anxieties and reasons to worry. We can become so preoccupied with daily stresses that all the joy and fun is sucked out of our lives.

We've already touched on the importance of smiling more at others because this causes our mirror neurons to trigger an impulse to smile back (Way 45). This way to be kind builds on that strong foundation by encouraging you to make sure that at least once a day you make a conscious effort to take yourself and others a little less seriously. Try to find ways to lighten the tone, enjoy the moment, see the funny side. By so doing, you might just help others feel lighter and brighter about themselves and life in general. Indeed, research[129] has shown that the science of humour is no laughing matter. Studies have shown it can ease stress and lower blood pressure and boost self-esteem and it does all this without any side effects. It heals lives and mends broken hearts and proves yet again the old adage that laughter really is the best medicine.

---

129   Louie, D. *et al.* (2016) 'The laughter prescription: A tool for lifestyle medicine.' *American Journal of Lifestyle Medicine*, 10(4) 262–267.

Take action

Ringmaster P.T. Barnum once said that the noblest art was to make others happy. Bear that in mind as you interact with the people in your lives. It starts with you not taking yourself too seriously. That lightness of spirit is truly infectious.

And if someone is having a tough time, endlessly reflecting on their problems and going around and around in circles may not be as helpful as doing something fun instead. Never underestimate the power of a good laugh, a new experience or a day out to lighten someone's load. It might help to think of fun and laughter in the same way as you think of sunshine – just as it would be unhealthy and damaging to stay indoors, curtains drawn and blocking out the light, so you need to let the fun and light into your life every day and as much as possible.

Bear in mind, too, that some of the most fun experiences are ones you can have for free, such as kicking the autumn leaves, running along a beach, jumping in puddles, laughing together when you watch a stand-up comedian or cooking together and producing disastrous results. There is a reason why that Gene Kelly song 'Singing in the Rain' is timeless and much loved. It's pouring. His suit is ruined. His shoes and socks are soaked, but he decides to dance in the rain anyway.

Remember, you always have a choice. You can huddle into a ball to shelter yourself or you can opt to dance whenever it rains.

Others – Way 69: Celebrate birthdays

If you are like most people, the older you get, the less concerned you become about your birthday. Birthday celebrations are big news for children and young adults but, as time goes on, the magic wears away and for older adults, it often feels like just another day. Indeed, time seems to speed up with age and a part of you may wish that your birthday didn't keep coming around so fast.

Fifteen years ago, I delved deep into the world of birthdays when I wrote a bestselling encyclopaedia of birthdays.[130] The book was written for adults and, over the years, became so popular that in 2020 I was asked to fully update and reissue it. One of the reasons for its popularity was that it reminded people of the potential of their birthday and what was special about that particular day and, by association, them. It brought some of the forgotten sparkle back to their birthdays and this way to be kinder to others is inspired by the power of birthdays. The endless messages from readers I have received have proved to me that whatever people say and however many times they tell you their birthday doesn't matter to them, that they don't want a fuss or don't mind if you forgot it, they do mind and their special day really does matter to them.

So, one of the kindest and most thoughtful things you can do for the people you really care about is to remember their birthday and wish them well.

Take action

If you are on a social media platform such as Facebook and your loved ones and friends are too, it is very easy to remember their birthdays – Facebook even reminds you. But not everybody is on Facebook and you may not be on it either. So, buy a small, inexpensive diary and write down the birthdays of the people who matter to you or of those you want to stay in touch with. Then, check that diary every day and when it is their birthday, send them a gift if appropriate and/or a card through the post, or, if that isn't possible, a text. Or call them. You don't have to say much more than 'Happy Birthday' but, trust me, as I'm a birth-

---

130 Cheung, T. (2007, reissued 2020) *The Element Encyclopedia of Birthdays* (reissued 2020 as *The Encyclopedia of Birthdays*). Harper Collins.

day guru, the fact that you have even remembered their birthday will make them feel good. It might even make their day. And if you feel brave enough you can always sing happy birthday on a voicemail or via FaceTime. During the lockdown, many people celebrated their birthdays in this way via Zoom or other platforms, showing how we found ways to be kind through continuing to mark and celebrate birthdays.

Of course, if people don't want to share their birthdate with you, respect that. But if you still want to celebrate them, write down their name and a date in your diary that you associate with them, such as when you first met or when something significant happened between you. Then, on that day, simply send them a text telling them how special they are to you and wish them a wonderful day.

Others – Way 70: Give festive cheer

Crisis helplines, such as the Samaritans, typically report[131] a high volume of calls on Christmas Day. It doesn't surprise me. Even though the festive period can be a tremendous opportunity to relax and enjoy special time with loved ones, whether people celebrate Christmas and are religious or not, for many it can be a lonely time. With its heavy emphasis on family, Christmas tends to bring up painful issues and memories. The pressure to spend, spend, spend or party, party, party can all get too much. Even if you are surrounded by people, you can feel very much alone at Christmas.

With that in mind, if you know someone who is alone this Christmas time, invite them around for a meal or a drink, or if you can't do that, send them a text or give them a call to let them know you are thinking of them. They may well refuse your invitation, but they will still really appreciate that you have thought of them during this special time of the year.

---

131 www.samaritans.org/news/samaritans-survey-reveals-festive-loneliness.

And if you are able to offer your time, charities and phone lines always need extra help and support on Christmas Day.

Take action

This Christmas, place kindness at the top of your wishlist. The build-up starts far too early for many of us – no sooner has Halloween passed than Christmas is upon us. Sadly, much of the tinsel and magic isn't about the compassionate spirit of Christmas, but simply to make us buy, buy, buy. So, recapture the true meaning and think of ways that you can help ease the stress of others during the festive season.

One way might be to refrain from sending cards, as that pressurises others to send them in return. Another is to donate the money you would spend on gifts to a good cause. But if you want to give people something really special at Christmas, give them your time and attention instead of material things.

And remember, too, that it's not just Christmas when people can feel extra-lonely. Valentine's Day is another very tough day for people who are alone, divorced or who have lost their partners. If you know of someone who may be feeling sad on that day, send them a text telling them how special they are, or you can even send them a card anonymously. It's amazing how good it feels to know you have a secret admirer.

Throughout the year, certain days may have special significance for the people you care about. Be sensitive to other religious holidays and occasions, as well as anniversaries, particularly those concerning departed loved ones. A kind word or a hello on those days can make all the difference. Many people haven't got anyone to turn to or have friends and family far away and need support. Knowing that you can be kind to such people, especially on the days when others are likely to be celebrating, is the best gift you can ever give – priceless.

Others – Way 71: Say their name

Dale Carnegie[132] – one of the world's most famous self-help authors – famously wrote that hearing your own name is the 'sweetest' and most 'important' sound. I've always loved using people's names when I speak to them and I've never been sure why, but there is a whole psychology to it. Reading or hearing your name makes you feel recognised, noticed, special as an individual and just as it gives you a lift when you use another person's name, it gives them a lift too. Other terms of endearment, such as 'love', although well meaning, really don't have the same impact because people tend to use them for everyone.

My first *Sunday Times* top-ten bestseller was called *An Angel Called My Name* and that title probably resonated because a person's name expresses their unique identity – who they truly are. It's a way to single someone out for special attention and to signal that you remember and have been paying attention to them. Have you ever been in that awkward situation when someone remembers your name, but you have completely forgotten theirs? You feel rude, even though you may have valid reasons for not remembering.

There is significant meaning and power in using someone's name when you speak to them. Not only does it make you feel more connected or close to the person, but it also makes them feel more focused on you. Above all, using someone's name makes them feel important. It isn't flattery, it's just a kind thing to do. So, this way to be kind encourages you to use people's names when you greet them or are in conversation with them. As for those other terms of endearment, only use them for complete strangers you are unlikely to meet again and only when appropriate – some people find being called 'darlin' by someone they don't know offensive.

---

132 Carnegie, D. (2012 re-issue) *How to Win Friends and Influence People.* Vermillion.

Take action

Perhaps you struggle to remember names? Although that may be true, the main reason people forget names is self-absorption. But whatever the reason, if you aren't good at remembering names, you can improve, regardless of your age or situation. Try the following technique.

When you meet someone new and they introduce themselves, repeat their name out loud and ask them whether you should call them that or if they have a preferred nickname or way of pronouncing their name. Next, ask them how their name is spelled, as there are often variations – for example, 'Claire' or 'Clare'. Then, whenever you talk to them, make a commitment to yourself to use their name at the beginning and the end of the conversation. And the same applies to online and email communications with them. Use their name.

There may still be times when you forget a name and, if that happens, apologise sincerely. The embarrassment of forgetting someone's name is a powerful incentive for it not to happen again. Never forget that everyone wants to be treated with respect. Using a person's name is a sign of your sincere desire to see them as the individual they truly are.

Others – Way 72: Respect your elders

Youth is venerated in our culture and for good reason, as the young have so much creativity and zest to offer the world. Young people are our future, so they need to be cherished and supported as much as possible, but it is important that our celebration of youth does not eclipse the older generations and the elderly. Sadly, a culture of dismissal of the elderly in society has overtaken the traditional veneration that defined previous generations. Once people are considered to be 'old', they can face rejection and loneliness. Research[133] shows that anxiety disorders among the elderly are becoming increasingly common today.

It's not just the elderly who are marginalised by the young and fit, either, because the same applies to the homeless, the sick, the disabled and others who are vulnerable. This way to be kind is mighty important because a person who does not respect or take care of the vulnerable is not a kind person, and a society that does not respect the fragile is a cruel one. One of the reasons some younger people don't show enough respect to the elderly is simply that they don't know where to start, so these suggestions offer guidelines to encourage them to take action.

An elderly person is still a person. Their body may be showing signs of age, but they were young once, too. They likely have experienced the same things as you are going through, so don't focus on the differences, focus on the similarities.

Older people can become set in their ways and that is their choice. Don't try to change them to suit your world view. You can offer help and advice and make suggestions. For example, encourage them to connect by video-calling the family if they miss seeing their loved ones, but if they don't want to do this for any reason, don't try to force them. Anyone who tries to impose their way of doing things onto others, automatically puts themselves into a superior position and that is disrespectful. What is new is not always better for everyone. Accept an elderly person for who they are. Hopefully, this will encourage them to accept you for who you are, too.

Take action

Listen to elderly people. They can offer tremendous insight and wisdom about life. They have lived through many experiences

---

133 Andreescu, C. & Lee, S. (2020) 'Anxiety disorders in the elderly.' *Advances in Experimental Medicine and Biology*, 1191, 561–576.

and typically have much of great value to communicate and pass on. Spend time with them and show empathy and tolerance for any physical limitations, such as loss of hearing or stiff fingers. Should there be signs of cognitive decline, again flex your empathy 'muscle' and consider how vulnerable they may be feeling. At all times, treat elderly people with the respect they deserve. If you see someone older struggling with bags or having trouble paying the parking meter, offer to help. Remind yourself that one day you will be old and vulnerable too.

Others – Way 73: Share food

Millions of people all around the world simply don't have enough food to eat. Even though we have more than enough food to go around, the sad truth, borne out by statistics,[134] shows that every day approximately one in nine people is hungry or, worse still, starving. And one in three suffers from some form of malnutrition.

These statistics are alarming, but the chances are that, if you are reading this book, you live in a country where the risk of death from starvation has largely been eradicated. These statistics won't feel as real or alarming to you as they should. But this way to be kind draws your attention to the sad and unjust fact that, even if you aren't aware of them, there are still millions of 'invisible' people in your country who go to bed each night feeling hungry and simply can't afford to buy nutritious food. One of the most humane things you can do for these people is to remember them and help. Feeding the hungry and finding ways to make donations to food banks whenever you get an opportunity is a powerful way to help those less fortunate than yourselves.

Kindness is essential for a better world, but never forget that to those who can't feed themselves and their families, it is also a luxury.

---

134 www.wfp.org/publications/2019-hunger-map.

Take action

Whenever you go food shopping, and if your funds allow, get into the habit of buying one or two extra non-perishable items. Collect them until you have a box full and then donate them to a food bank. Countless people rely on food banks for their survival. If you don't know where your local food bank is, many supermarkets have collection points you can use for donations.

When giving items to a food bank, do ensure the contents are nutritious and, most important of all, non-perishable. Here are the items recommended as the ideal donations by the Trussell Trust food banks in the UK:

- Cereal
- Soup
- Pasta
- Rice
- Tinned tomatoes/pasta sauce
- Lentils, beans and pulses
- Tinned meat
- Tinned vegetables
- Tea/coffee
- Tinned fruit
- Biscuits
- UHT milk
- Fruit juice.

Remember also that non-food items are also needed by food banks, for example:

- Toiletries: deodorant, toilet paper, shower gel, shaving gel, shampoo, soap, toothbrushes, toothpaste, hand wipes

- Household items: laundry liquid detergent, laundry powder, washing-up liquid
- Feminine hygiene products: sanitary towels and tampons
- Baby supplies: nappies, baby wipes and baby food (but not formula milk due to UNICEF regulations).

You may also wish to organise a fundraising event for your local food bank or, better still, volunteer to help package and deliver food at a food bank.

And remember the 'giving through food' theme the next time you pass a homeless person in the street begging for money. Instead of throwing your spare change at them, see if you can use it to buy them a cup of tea or coffee and a sandwich instead.

Others – Way 74: Do something for nothing

The 2020 pandemic lockdown closed shops, cafes and services to try to help prevent the spread of infection. Many of us remained at home for extended periods of time, unable to work and doing without all those things we thought were essential, such as trips to restaurants, hairdressers and beauticians. It was a shock to the system but, if there was any silver lining, it taught us just how much money we had been wasting on things that don't really matter.

I myself realised how much money I had been spending unnecessarily on getting my nails done and going to coffee shops. In my books[135] I have always maintained that the most priceless things in life are free, and the lockdown certainly underlined the truth of that when I rediscovered the joys of simply laughing, going for walk alone and watching the sun set, reading a good book, listening to great music, and so on. But I also noticed how much I had been spending on others. So, instead of splashing out

135 Cheung, T. (2020) *The Sensitivity Code.* Thread.

on gifts for them or taking them out for meals or to the cinema, which was no longer viable or possible, I had to think of ways to be kind that didn't involve cash – namely giving them my time, energy, creativity, attention and heart instead.

Take action

Kick-start being kind without expense by de-cluttering your living and workspace. Then, give away or donate for free anything you no longer need but others can still use. After that, think of other, imaginative ways to be kind. Make, rather than buy, cards for loved ones, cook family meals from scratch, bake cakes and biscuits for others. If you have musical talent, sing or play for them. If you love gardening, help someone tend to their plants and flowers. Wash someone's car or dishes. Offer to go to the shops for a friend or neighbour, or to walk their dog. If you have a skill, share it for free. If everyone did that, the world would be a kinder place. In fact, doing something without charging is behind a remarkable online movement currently inspiring millions all over the world. Called #DoSomethingForNothing,[136] it was founded by Joshua Coombes, a hairdresser who started to give free haircuts to street people.

The possibilities to help others for free are endless. Ask around and find out who needs help and, before you know it, you'll be enjoying their surprised yet delighted reaction when they receive your offer.

If you have cash to spare, of course, treating loved ones and donating to good causes is still a wonderful way to be kinder to others, but never forget the lesson of the lockdown. So many things we spend money on, thinking we are helping others, are not necessary or even memorable. The most generous thing you can ever give others costs nothing – the gift of your time and attention.

---

136 www.pointsoflight.gov.uk/do-something-for-nothing.

Others – Way 75: Treat others as equals

Have you ever had someone patronise or talk down to you? Perhaps you have experienced the opposite, and someone has been overly subservient?

Even though you might prefer others to look up to you rather than down on you, both approaches can be unsettling and have an alienating effect, as they put you in a different class or category to the person you are speaking to.

It's human nature to compare ourselves to others, but research has shown that the comparison game is a source of great unhappiness. One of the reasons social media use has been linked with increased risk of depression in several recent studies[137] is because the platforms encourage users to compare themselves and their lives with others. These comparisons prompt people to think of themselves as either superior or inferior to others. It doesn't really matter which, as any kind of comparison increases the risk of anxiety and sadness. It's really positive that some platforms are now taking steps to stop the online comparison 'disease' by removing the 'like' option, but it's also important that you take steps to avoid the comparison trap in your interactions with others.

This way to be kinder to others encourages you to treat other people as equals. The only person you should be comparing yourself to is the person you were yesterday. Considering yourself better or worse than anyone else is an act of unkindness towards both others and yourself. Moving forward, any time you find yourself making comparisons in a way that diminishes either them or you, divert that energy into taking better care of yourself and your own needs. There is nothing wrong with admiring others for what they do, but not at the cost of your own self-esteem. Let the success of others inspire you to take the steps to do what you need to do and

---

137 Pera, A. (2018) 'Psychological processes involved in social comparison, depression, and envy on Facebook.' *Frontiers in Psychology*, 9 22.

be whoever you want to be, and if you find yourself thinking you are better than anyone else, take a reality check. Feeling superior comes from a position of fear, not true self-confidence.

Take action

Social media can be wonderfully motivating, informative and inspirational, but if you are falling into the comparison trap, you may think it's best to do a social media detox for a while to focus on your own life and decide where you are heading.

In your interactions with others, remember to focus on what you have in common as human beings and remind yourself that everyone is on their own journey in this life. Nobody is better or worse than anyone else, just different. Comparing yourself up or down doesn't help make you, others or the world a kinder place. It just gives away your power, destroys rather than creates, and triggers uncertainty or separation from others. From now on, focus on looking straight ahead, being the best that you can be, seeing the best in others and what unites rather than divides human beings from each other.

Others – Way 76: Agree to disagree

The temptation to think that others should always see our viewpoint or do what we feel is the best thing flares up in us all from time to time. Obviously, losing your temper isn't the answer because that isn't going to change anyone's mind, it is just going to increase your stress levels[138] and make you feel unwell. Trying to change someone's mind isn't advisable either, because people like to make up their own minds. But what do you do if someone

---

138 Staicu, M.L. *et al.* (2010) 'Anger and health risk behaviours.' *Journal of Medicine and Life*, 15; 3(4) 372–375.

stubbornly disagrees with you or is offensive or irritating and you arrive at an impasse? What is the kind thing to do? Should you try to hold your ground? Should you walk away? Should you let them have their way?

The kind thing is to forgive yourself and others whenever there is dissonance, because forgiveness boosts your mood and wellbeing, and the mood and wellbeing of others.[139] Forgiving isn't the same as agreeing or endorsing and it's more than letting go or moving on. True forgiveness is offering something positive – empathy, compassion, understanding – to the person who disagrees with or hurts you. It is finding common ground if you can and, if you can't, gracefully agreeing to disagree.

Take action

When you find yourself at loggerheads with someone or in real disagreement with their viewpoint, don't let anger or silence take over. Anger just separates you further and can also seriously damage your health and wellbeing. It also encourages the other person to respond in kind and is just as bad for others as it is for you. The silent treatment or not discussing or acknowledging there is an issue isn't helpful either, because it simply pushes the problem underground, where it festers and inevitably resurfaces when triggered, perhaps stronger than before.

The kinder way forward is to understand that disagreement has a creative element in that both of you can learn new perspectives from different approaches or opinions and, from these new perspectives, you can both find original solutions. Also remind yourself that the world would be very boring if everyone agreed all the time.

So, when someone disagrees with you, try to see their perspective and find common ground by acknowledging the strength of

---

139 Toussaint, L.L. *et al.* (2015) *Forgiveness and Health: Scientific Evidence and Theories Relating Forgiveness to Better Health.* Springer.

their conviction. We all like to think we are right and so, if you then still disagree with them, agree to disagree. If the argument continues, say you are sorry they feel that way and be the first to walk away, perhaps saying something kind like, 'I don't share your opinion, but I'm really grateful you have explained it to me.' And if that person continues to disrespect you, do yourself the biggest favour of all and let go. Release them from your life or limit your interaction with them if you can't block them. Contrary to what you may believe, not giving up on toxic people and keeping them in your life in the hope they will see your worth and change is a recipe for disaster. In the great majority of cases when someone shows you who they are, believe them. Value yourself enough to walk away.

The art of agreeing to disagree is underrated. But it is one of the kindest and most healing ways to respond to other people in our lives whenever there is disagreement or unresolved tension.

Others – Way 77: Experience the 'Roseto effect'

The kind thing to do when you see someone struggling with their bags is to offer to help carry them; or when the person in the queue behind you has one or two items but you have a full trolley, to let them go ahead of you. Doing the kind thing may require conscious effort if you are preoccupied and busy yourself, but the rewards make it very worthwhile. Next time you practise an act of unprompted kindness for a fellow human being, notice how it makes you feel. You initially feel good about yourself, and then you notice you're experiencing what scientists call the 'Roseto effect', which makes you feel calmer and more relaxed.

The Roseto effect is a term coined in the 1960s by researchers who examined a population of Italians living in Roseto, a small town in Pennsylvania, USA. The reason for the study, which was funded by the American state and federal governments, was to discover why people in the Roseto community rarely suffered from heart disease. The study confirmed the low incidence of heart disease in the community and went on to examine why this was the case. What they discovered became known as the Roseto effect.

The researchers first looked at what people in Roseto were eating to see if that played a part, but the immigrant community's diet wasn't the reason. They then examined other factors, from the water supply to their religious beliefs, but no connection was found. And then they studied family relationships and people's sense of community – and they hit the jackpot. The people in Roseto shared close community bonds and this lowered their stress levels and protected their hearts. Thirty years later, when the immigrant community had become more Americanised and insular, a further study[140] confirmed that rates of mortality from heart disease had risen. The conclusion was that people in communities where they help and look out for each other are healthier and happier.

This way to be kinder encourages you to keep an eye out for the wellbeing of others wherever you are.

Take action

Don't reserve acts of kindness just for people you know or work with. As much as possible, embody the Roseto effect wherever you go and whoever you interact with, especially in your local neighbourhood or community. Notice what is going on around you and, if you see someone in need of help, don't hesitate to offer it. Doing that will encourage a much-needed sense of community. If others notice you being kind to someone else, they are more likely to be kinder to others themselves. During the lockdown, many local community bonds were strengthened by simple acts of kindness, such as saying hello to people

---

140 Egolf, B. *et al.* (1992) 'The Roseto effect: A 50-year comparison of mortality rates.' *American Journal of Public Health*, 82(8) 1089–1092.

in the street or leaving food outside the door of a vulnerable neighbour.

If you meet resistance, politely back away and understand that the person you have offered to help has their reasons to decline. Simply offering to help – even if it is not accepted – is what truly matters here, because by offering you have shown kindness and set the right tone.

Others – Way 78: Be a good Samaritan

It's one thing agreeing to disagree and doing the kind thing when others are being offensive or unfair towards you, but what do you do when you witness someone being attacked or treated unjustly? Should you intervene or should you assume that the person is perfectly capable of fighting their own battle?

The chances are that if you care about the person, your instinct is to intervene on their behalf. That is perfectly understandable, but what if the person being harassed is a total stranger?

The way we react when someone we don't know is being treated unfairly or harassed seems to be governed by their appearance. Research has shown that we are more likely to intervene to help those who appear similar to ourselves, perhaps because they are from a similar background or ethnic or cultural group. Few people are willing to help complete strangers or people they make negative assumptions about. One study,[141] on a New York subway, involved a person collapsing while holding either a cane or a bottle of alcohol. Help was offered to the person carrying the cane, but only in 50 per cent of cases to the person carrying alcohol.

This way to be kind encourages you to be a good Samaritan and not a disinterested passer-by, and to help others who urgently

---

141 Pilavin, I.M. *et al.* (1969) 'Good Samaritanism: An underground
     phenomenon.' *Journal of Personality and Social Psychology*, 13(4) 289–299.

need help, regardless of their appearance or any assumptions you may make about them.

Take action

If you witness someone in trouble or being intimidated, the kindest thing to do is to offer to help. Don't just walk on by – although your safety is key and you should never put yourself in any danger. If you notice someone who has fallen over, is struggling or is being harassed, make contact and offer to help them or stand up for them.

It's always best to speak to the person who is in trouble or is being treated offensively first, rather than to wade in uninvited or to challenge the harassers. Ask them if they need any help and, if you witness foul play, do all you safely can to create space between them and the person intimidating them. If it isn't safe for you to help or intervene, immediately report the incident to the authorities or the police. The same applies if you hear about intimidation of any kind at work, in your community or your school. Seek out the victims and ask them if they need help. If that isn't possible or they are defensive, report what you know to the authorities, anonymously if necessary.

Whatever you do, don't ignore obvious wrongdoing. Be a strong spokesperson for those who can't defend themselves. In the immortal words of Martin Luther King, 'Our lives begin to end the day we become *silent* about things that matter' and 'The ultimate tragedy is not the oppression and cruelty by the bad people but the *silence* over that by the good people.'

Others – Way 79: Help the homeless

In an ideal world, there would be no homeless people. But the world isn't an ideal place and there are thousands and thousands of people in almost every country around the world who, for whatever reason, don't have a place to shelter or live in. The streets are their home. Recent surveys[142] suggest that up to 2 per cent of the global population has no home. It's impossible for any decent human being to walk past a homeless person or a beggar without feeling some concern, empathy and, perhaps, curiosity. You may imagine what someone's life must be like and wonder what has reduced them to such strained circumstances.

Perhaps you routinely reach into your pocket or bag every time you pass them and throw them some change. Or perhaps you believe that giving them money isn't helpful because they are likely to spend it on drink or drugs. Or maybe you always hurry past them, pretending they are invisible and avoiding eye contact because it makes you feel so uncomfortable. In short, you aren't sure how you can help the homeless or what is the best or kindest thing to do.

This way to be kind explains the most effective ways to help homeless people.

Take action

Homeless shelters are always in need of volunteers all year round to help feed and take care of their guests. They get inundated with offers to help at Christmas, but receive fewer during the rest of the year, so do offer your time regularly to help, if you can.

If volunteering isn't for you, the kindest thing to do whenever you pass a homeless person is to alert professionals who can direct them to a shelter or a refuge. For example, in the UK, there's StreetLink, an organisation you can call or contact via an app to report the location of a homeless person. They will then try to find the person and see if they can help. Many homeless people don't know there are resources out there to help them find food

---

142 https://yaleglobal.yale.edu/content/cities-grow-so-do-numbers-homeless.

and shelter, or they are so weak they no longer know what's the best way to help themselves.

Giving them your spare change comes from noble intentions, but it is far better to offer them food or drinks, blankets or clothing rather than money. Things that can take away their hunger and keep them warm are priorities and, if they also have a dog – and many do have loyal canine companions – you can offer them dog food and blankets too.

Never underestimate the importance and kindness of engaging with a homeless person. If someone is sleeping rough, try not to judge them but to regard them as simply a human being who has fallen on hard times. They have a beating heart, just like you. So, smile and say hello. If you feel brave enough, and it is safe to do so, engage them in conversation. You might just find that all your assumptions about homeless people are changed for ever.

Others – Way 80: Count the ways

As we have seen from the pay it forward effect, your kindness to-wards others encourages those who benefit from it to be kinder, in turn, to the people in their own lives. Research[143] has clearly proved that not only can being kind make you feel great, but also observing or hearing about kindness towards others can create a positive ripple effect by encouraging the production of those kindness-induced feel-good hormones, such as oxytocin and se-rotonin, that increase feelings of self-esteem and optimism and make you more likely to want to be kind. If you've ever wanted to make a difference but felt that your life wasn't going in the direction you would like it to go in, being kinder to others is the perfect way to find purpose and ensure your life matters. That's why this final way to be kinder to others encourages you to keep

---

143 www.randomactsofkindness.org/the-science-of-kindness.

your eyes and your heart open and to notice or find ways to be kinder to others every day and as often as possible from now on.

Don't let a day go past again without seeking an opportunity to showcase the power of kindness in all your interactions with others. Although this is your eightieth way to be kinder, when it comes to seeking out ways to be kinder to others, let yourself count the ways. Or better still, lose count and make being kind to others who you are, and random acts of kindness your way of life.

Take action

Never ignore the power of kindness on the people you interact with in your life. Kindness heals and saves lives. There are endless ways to be kind, but if you need more suggestions as well as the ones already given, here are some ideas for more random acts of kindness to help you keep on making a difference every day.

- Smile and say hello to a stranger.
- Hold the door open for the person behind you.
- Make someone a cup of tea or coffee without asking them first.
- Compliment a parent or a pet owner on their child or pet.
- Encourage others to succeed and look for the best in them.
- Provide a shoulder to cry on.
- Help someone by running errands for them.
- Help someone who is struggling with their luggage.
- Send a photo memory to a friend.
- Write to thank a teacher who inspired you.
- Put back a neighbour's wheelie bin.
- Say sorry.
- Make everyone feel included.
- Help someone clean up a mess.
- Be happy for someone else's success.

- Share something you love.
- Leave a generous tip if you can.
- Give way at a junction.
- Compliment a stranger.
- Leave inspirational notes in public places.
- Invite someone who is lonely for a meal.
- Offer to take a picture for someone.
- Leave unwanted books or newspapers and magazines in waiting rooms or on public transport.
- Say thank you.
- Tell someone you love and value them.

Your aim is to make being kinder and more considerate to others second nature to you and an intrinsic part of your everyday life. The more kindness for others you carry out, the more that kindness will become your automatic response and the more you will become the change you want to see in the world.

CHAPTER 5

20 WAYS TO BE KINDER TO NATURE

Love the world as your own self; then you can truly care for all things. Lao Tzu

Being kinder to nature – taking better care of the natural world and the resources that sustain us – isn't just the necessary and responsible thing to do to help save the planet, it's the kindest thing you can do for your own emotional, mental and physical health and wellbeing. In recent decades, there has been an increasing trend towards spending more and more of our lives inside and online, and the 2020 pandemic lockdown likely accelerated this disturbing trend. It's disturbing because science[144] has proved over and over again that spending time in nature can ease stress and boost immunity, creativity, concentration and your willingness and ability to connect with generosity to others.

Cutting yourself off from nature makes you less likely to be kind to yourself and others. It seems that the awe and sense of connection with something greater than yourself that you feel whenever you see natural beauty – whether that be a stunning

---

144 White, M.P. *et al.* (2019) 'Spending at least 120 minutes a week in nature is associated with good health and wellbeing.' *Scientific Reports, 9,* 7730. https://doi.org/10.1038/s41598-019-44097-3.

sunset, a shimmering lake, a gorgeous butterfly, a colourful autumn leaf, a glittering rainbow or the sparkle of the stars at night – has a positive impact not just on you but on the world. This is because whenever you feel awe, you are more far more likely to be generous to others. In a nutshell, if more of us spent time appreciating natural beauty and wildlife, the world would become a far more compassionate place.

If you require any more convincing that you should spend more time in nature, remind yourself that centuries ago we were born in natural settings and our survival would depend on how tuned into nature we were. This ancient longing to connect with nature remains in our DNA. It is sad that in our technology-dependent, materialistic, urban-centric world, nature is marginalised, and it really doesn't make sense, given the volume of research that points to the holistic wellbeing benefits of connecting to nature.

Health professionals are increasingly concerned about the growth in Nature Deficit Disorder,[145] which can be especially harmful to children. A cluster of research studies[146] has linked a number of health conditions, such as obesity and depression, as well as loss of concentration and creativity, to disconnection with nature. These studies have inspired and support the life-enhancing, kindness-boosting benefits of the suggestions that follow. Although nature isn't a cure-all, the more you experience it and appreciate it, the healthier and happier you are likely to feel and the kinder you are going to want to be towards yourself and others. Indeed, there is even research[147] to suggest that spending time in nature

145 Warber, S. *et al.* (2015) 'Addressing "Nature-Deficit Disorder": A mixed methods pilot study of young adults attending a wilderness camp.' *Evidence-Based Complementary and Alternative Medicine*, 2015: 651827.

146 www.health.harvard.edu/mind-and-mood/sour-mood-getting-you-down-get-back-to-nature.

147 Piff, P.K. *et al.* (2015) 'Awe, the small self, and prosocial behavior.' *Journal of Personality and Social Psychology, 108*(6) 883–899.

itself makes you kinder. So, with every act of kindness towards nature, you are helping to make the world a kinder place.

I have personal experience of the healing benefits of nature. Whenever I have felt overwhelmed, sad or alone for whatever reason, taking time out in a natural setting or simply spending time with my little dog, Arnie, has always brought me a fresh perspective and hope. Twenty years ago, I upended my life and made the decision to move away from the city and live right beside a forest. I have never once regretted it. Feeling close to nature and trees when I wake up every morning brings me comfort and inspiration, and a sense of connection with everyone and everything.

Of course, living close to nature isn't possible for everyone and many of us live mainly indoor lives, so that's why the first ten ways to be kinder to nature highlight ways to enhance your personal connection with nature. The remaining ten ways to be kinder to nature then focus on specific things you can do to be kinder to the planet. All 20 ways can help you bring the wonder, joy and inspiration of nature – and its proven ability to inspire compassion towards yourself and others – into your heart, your relationships and the world.

It's really very simple. The kinder you are towards the Earth and the more connected you feel to nature, the kinder you are likely to be towards yourself and others and the kinder the world becomes. Kind people value and respect nature.

Nature – Way 81: Try 'earthing'

I'm starting this section with a suggestion that can immediately help you feel a connection again with the Earth, especially if you are feeling cut off from it. You are going to do some barefoot walking on grass, mud or sand.

As a child, you likely ran around barefoot in your garden or the park, but can you remember when you last felt the earth beneath your feet? Barefoot walking is incredibly therapeutic because the Earth is a source of living energy and when your soles come into direct contact with that energy, you can absorb it into your body, mind and soul. If this all sounds a little too 'New Age' for you to experiment with, I'd like you to know that scientists have studied the therapeutic[148] mood and health benefits of walking barefoot and found them to be so promising they have a technical term for it: 'earthing'.[149]

Take action

Take a small towel or a blanket and go outside. Find some soft grass, mud or sand in your garden, or at your local park or beach. Be sure to check that there are no sharp objects lying around, by doing a trial run with your shoes on first. Then, remove your shoes and socks and walk for at least five minutes on the grass or natural surface. You can walk around in circles if the area you have picked is small. The important thing is that you pay mindful attention to how it feels to have direct contact with nature in this way. Savour the reconnection. Focus your attention on each step and how each one feels different because just as every human being is unique, so is every blade of grass, patch of mud and grain of sand.

If you feel embarrassed or silly at any point, recall the scientific research that proves the therapeutic value. After five minutes, wipe your feet with your towel, put your shoes and socks back on and

---

148 Oschman, J. *et al.* (2015) 'The effects of earthing on inflammation, the immune response wound healing and prevention and treatment of chronic inflammatory and autoimmune diseases.' *Journal of Inflammation Research*, 8 83–96.

149 Chevalier, G. *et al.* (2012) 'Earthing: health implications of reconnecting the human body to the earth's surface electrons.' *Journal of Environmental and Public Health*, 2012: 291541.

return to your day, knowing that you are taking the natural healing energy of the Earth, which you've just absorbed through the soles of your feet, with you. Be sure to wash your feet before you walk around barefoot in your home or go to bed. If you are feeling more connected to the Earth and notice how this boosts your mood, health and desire to be more compassionate, you might want to make earthing something you do regularly, perhaps extending the time you walk barefoot to ten or more minutes.

Note: If you have any cuts on your feet, plaster them or wait until they heal before trying earthing.

Nature – Way 82: Watch the skies

An enjoyable way to feel connected to nature and to remind yourself that you a part of the Earth and its wonders is to do some cloud-watching. Clouds are very familiar to us and we often take them for granted, but spending time regularly gazing at the skies above in wonder is an incredibly inspiring way to foster a genuine sense of connection with the natural world.

Cloud-spotting is something you probably did in your childhood. Remember lying in the grass watching the shapes shift and transform? It was mesmerising and relaxing. But as you got older, cloud-watching likely became a thing of the past. What you may not realise is that mindfully gazing at the clouds is a brilliant way to feel connected to nature again, because it is impossible not to feel a sense of awe and interconnectedness when you study the shifting shapes above you. Feelings of natural awe have been shown to make people kinder,[150] and watching clouds is also a form of natural meditation, known to ease stress.

---

150 https://scienceline.org/2016/06/watching-the-clouds-go-by.

Take action

To do your cloud-watching, simply sit beside a window with a view of the sky, but obviously do it outside if you can, preferably lying on your back on the ground.

Set a timer for ten minutes, as it is easy to lose track of time when you are watching clouds. Make yourself comfortable and gaze up at the sky. If the sun is out, don't look at it directly. Don't stare intently at the clouds, just look at them gently in the same way you might look at scenery as you walk. Note any shapes you see and the sense of expanded awareness this exercise gives you. Notice how it reminds you that you are part of nature, something bigger than yourself. When the ten minutes are up, yawn, stretch and blink your eyes several times to reconnect to your everyday life.

The ancient druids believed that clouds could offer guidance, but whether or not that is the case, cloud-watching and studying the shapes and formations of the clouds above you is a fun and highly absorbing way to reconnect with nature. You may even find yourself talking to the clouds, as your mind wanders. The American philosopher and poet Henry Thoreau found that talking to clouds motivated him, so don't hold back – you are in fine company. And don't stop at cloud-watching: if you ever get an opportunity to watch the sun rise or set, as recommended in the self-kindness section, you can experience the same transformative impact on your body, mind, heart and soul. Sunrises and sunsets are the greatest shows on Earth. As with cloud-watching, there is research[151] to show that watching the sun rise and set can change you for the better by encouraging you to feel more grateful and to be more generous to others.

---

151 Zhang, J. *et al.* (2014) 'Engagement with natural beauty moderates the positive reaction between connectedness with nature and psychological well-being.' *Journal of Environmental Psychology*, 38, 55–63.

Nature – Way 83: As above, so below

The next time you feel overwhelmed, confused or angry after a hard day, go outside and spend a few moments gazing up at the night sky. This won't solve all your problems instantly, but it will give you some much-needed perspective and calm.

Research[152] shows stargazing can make you kinder because it diminishes self-interest and promotes a desire to improve the welfare of others. There is nothing like gazing at a starlit night sky to make your personal problems feel insignificant. You instinctively sense that, in the grand scheme of things, your stresses are not important. This shift in perspective brings humility and encourages you to be kinder and to seek common ground with others.

The more stargazing you do, the more compassionate and invested you are likely to become in helping others or saving the planet. You may even sense that life is short and decide to spend your precious time making a difference by serving the greater good.

Take action

You may think that stargazing is a skill you need to learn or that it requires complicated equipment, but this is not the case. Stargazing is for everyone and you can do it any time the stars come out to shine.

When it gets dark enough, go outside. Always make sure you are safe and don't go anywhere isolated by yourself. Bring your mobile phone or a torch with you so you can see where you are going, if necessary. Your garden is ideal, but you can also just stand outside. If you prefer to stay indoors, a window with a clear view of the night sky will suffice.

Once you have found a spot with a good view of the night sky, take a few deep breaths. It may take ten minutes for your eyes to

---

152 Piff, P. *et al.* (2015) 'Awe, the small self, and prosocial behavior.' *Journal of Personality and Social Psychology*, 108(6) 883–899.

adjust if it is very dark. Then, gently look up at the heavens above and gaze mindfully at the stars. Don't think about anything, just observe them shining down on you. If you start to feel yourself merging with them, allow yourself to do so. Gaze at them for five to ten minutes and then, when you are ready, lower your head, take some more deep breaths and silently thank the stars for being there every single night.

Be aware that some nights are cloudy, so you may want to wait for a clear starry night before stargazing. Remember, though, that even if you can't see the stars clearly, like the sun, the moon, the planets and the eternity of space, they are always there. The best time to stargaze is when the moon is dark or new, as the light of the full moon can be too distracting.

Nature – Way 84: Nurture a plant

Biophilia is the term used to describe changing our homes and work environments to more closely resemble the natural world. Studies[153] have shown that biophilic features can significantly boost mood and health. Even more promising, research also shows[154] they can increase altruistic behaviour. You may not re-alise it but ensuring there are living plants and natural features in your home and workplace can not only boost your wellbeing but also make you and others living and working there kinder.

This way to be kind asks you to bring a house plant into your home. It's an especially beneficial thing to do if your life is based indoors, or you don't have a garden or live close to a park or a

153 Park, S.H. *et al.* (2009) 'Ornamental indoor plants in hospital rooms enhanced health outcomes of patients recovering from surgery.' *Journal of Alternative and Complementary Medicine*, 15(9) 975–980.

154 Guéguen, N. (2016) '"Green Altruism": short immersion in natural green environments and helping behavior.' *Environment and Behavior*, 48(2) 324–342.

natural space. If you worry that you don't have time to care for a plant, there are plenty of very low-maintenance ones that are very easy to care for. Cacti or spider plants are ideal because they are so easy to nurture, along with Chinese evergreens and dracaenas. English ivy is believed to be optimum for air filtering. If you are still reluctant, remind yourself that green plants help purify and humidify the air and bring some of the natural health-boosting benefits of nature right into your home.

Take action

Purchase or borrow a plant. It really doesn't matter what that plant is and it need not be expensive; just ensure that it is an indoor plant and preferably a green one, as they have been shown to offer the most benefits for humidifying and purifying the air. You may wish to rescue a wilting plant that has been discounted in a garden centre.

Find a spot in your home or workspace where you can see your new plant every day. You can place it on a windowsill if it needs light, but make sure you follow the care instructions and feed, water and nurture your plant as instructed. Each day spend time – it only needs to be a few moments – studying your plant and taking care that it has all it needs to thrive. As you tend it, give it your full attention and send it gratitude for the health benefits it is giving you and the loving connection with nature it fosters within you. If you already own plants in your home or workspace, recommit to taking care of them with renewed enthusiasm.

Don't feel you have to restrict yourself to just one plant. The more bonds with living plants and flowers you have in your home and your life, the better. Notice how bringing living plants indoors can help boost your health, mood and make you and everyone you open your door to a little kinder.

Nature – Way 85: Find your roots

Spending more time in nature reminds you that everyone and everything is connected and that all plants, trees and flowers are alive, just as you are. Forests and trees are teeming with life, and are essential for our health and wellbeing, but they are being destroyed at an alarming rate today. When you feel more connected to nature, you may just find that you start to feel the pain of this loss and want to take an active part in saving trees and forests from destruction.

Perhaps one of the most healing and wonderful ways to connect better with nature and reap the benefits is to head for the forest. This way to be kinder encourages you to tune into the natural world by visiting and spending time mindfully in a wood or a forest or, if that isn't possible, finding a tree to lean against. Or better still, consider planting or adopting a tree. Remember trees are living things and they need kindness, love and nurturing just as much as you do and everyone else does.

Take action

The Japanese practice of forest bathing has been shown[155] to significantly reduce stress and improve mood, health and overall wellbeing. Studies, primarily from Japan, show that there are tremendous holistic health, immune, concentration and mood boosting as well as stress-reduction benefits to spending time close to trees. Shinrin-Yoku, translated into English as 'forest bathing', means drinking in the forest atmosphere while taking a mindful walk there. It was developed as a healing therapy in Japan in the 1980s, and has become an established part of preventative healthcare there.

---

155 Wen, Y. *et al.* (2019) 'Medical empirical research on forest bathing (*Shinrin-yoku*): A systematic review.' *Environmental Health and Preventative Medicine*, 24, 70. https://doi.org/10.1186/s12199-019-0822-8.

So, set aside a couple of hours to visit a wood or a forest and immerse yourself in the green scenery. If you are going alone, remember that safety is your number one concern, so don't go anywhere too remote, let someone know where you are and take your phone with you.

On arrival, switch off all notifications on your phone and just wander through the trees. Don't walk briskly or energetically, simply amble along. This isn't about exercise but reconnecting to nature through your senses. As you walk, let your mind wander too and, if thoughts start to intrude, remind yourself of the proven benefits of forest bathing. When you are ready, find a tree that you feel drawn to and simply sit under it. Lean your back against the tree and feel yourself connect to its wisdom. Absorb the sights, smells and sounds around you and taste the fresh air. Listen to the birds singing and feel the breeze. Simply notice all the life forms around you. When you feel ready, say goodbye to your tree with gratitude and respect and wander back through the forest to your starting point.

If forest bathing isn't for you, just find a tree to tune into and lean on. And when you feel your connection with trees growing, either adopt or plant a tree. One of the kindest gifts you can give yourself or someone you care about is the gift of a tree. Having a tree planted in your name feels special and if you also do this for a loved one, you not only make them feel special but are also doing something positive and kind for the planet.

Nature – Way 86: Talk to plants

Nature lovers will immediately understand what I am saying here. When you spend time in a natural setting, it can often feel as if nature is talking to you – in a completely different language, of course. A language that doesn't use words, but a language all the same.

The Romantic poets Wordsworth, Coleridge and Keats immersed themselves in the natural world and saw nature as a teacher, a communicator. Many of their poems attempt to describe this dialogue between humankind and nature. Here's one of the most famous poems by Wordsworth – it's all about a conversation with nature:

> I wandered lonely as a cloud
> That floats on high o'er vales and hills,
> When all at once I saw a crowd,
> A host, of golden daffodils;
> Beside the lake, beneath the trees,
> Fluttering and dancing in the breeze.
>
> Continuous as the stars that shine
> And twinkle on the milky way,
> They stretched in never-ending line
> Along the margin of a bay:
> Ten thousand saw I at a glance,
> Tossing their heads in sprightly dance.
>
> The waves beside them danced; but they
> Out-did the sparkling waves in glee:
> A poet could not but be gay,
> In such a jocund company:
> I gazed—and gazed—but little thought
> What wealth the show to me had brought:
>
> For oft, when on my couch I lie
> In vacant or in pensive mood,
> They flash upon that inward eye
> Which is the bliss of solitude;
> And then my heart with pleasure fills,
> And dances with the daffodils.

What Wordsworth is describing here is the communication between himself and the natural world. The chances are you have felt this too yet dismissed it as all in your imagination. But as the Romantic poets articulated, talking to and listening to nature – feeling that two-way connection – is completely normal and natural. Indeed, feeling a living connection to nature is called animism[156] and is a common feature among ancient and indigenous cultures. A recent study by the Royal Horticultural Society[157] showed that there is a connection between talking to plants and their healthier growth. So, if you want to be kinder to nature, talk to her!

Take action

Go outside and find a natural spot. Tune in and listen to your senses. What do you feel? What do you hear? What do you smell? If you hear beautiful sounds, talk back either silently or out loud. If there are unpleasant smells, sense what they are saying to you, too. Then start conversing with nature silently or out loud.

If you feel uncomfortable doing this outside, try talking to your indoor plants or the flowers in your garden. Prince Charles talks to his plants, so you are in good company. Every time you communicate with nature you are connecting to your inner wisdom. You are nature. Nature is who you are. Make sure you have a wonderful conversation.

Nature – Way 87: Love animals

One of the most obvious ways to be kinder to nature is to be kinder to animals. Whether as pets or food sources, animals save

---

156 Stringer, M.D. (1999) 'Rethinking animism: Thoughts from the infancy of our discipline.' *Journal of the Royal Anthropological Institute*, 5(4) 541–556. doi:10.2307/2661147

157 http://news.bbc.co.uk/1/hi/uk/7973727.stm.

and heal lives. We owe them our gratitude and respect. Our ancestors sensed and celebrated the interconnection between ourselves and animals, and this way to be kinder to nature encourages you to open up your heart to animals.

All animals have feelings – even fish can feel. Aside from respecting and expressing gratitude for those that give their lives to feed and clothe us, we should also value the healing power of the animals that share our lives. Studies[158] show that a pet can ease stress and depression, and boost mood. As a dog and cat owner, I know that to be a fact. Pets helps you live in the moment and they love you regardless of how you look or feel, which is terrific for self-esteem. They are also amazing company if you live alone, and walking your dog is a great incentive to exercise. Simply stroking a cat or a dog releases feel-good hormones. That's why animal-assisted therapy is often used in hospitals and hospices, and why giving dogs to prisoners can aid their rehabilitation.

Over the years, I have lost count of all the wonderful stories I have received from readers about pets healing and transforming lives. But it's not just pets, wild animals can also offer comfort and inspiration. If you have ever gone for a walk in the woods and spotted a deer that stared silently back at you, you will know how mesmerising it feels to connect with a wild animal.

Take action

Animals are living, feeling beings. The way you treat them says a lot about who you are. Kind people uniformly treat animals kindly, too. If you own a pet, treasure the moments you have with them – they are with us for such a short time. If you can't or don't want to own a pet and are not vegetarian or vegan, send

158 Brooks, H.L. *et al.* (2018) 'The power of support from companion animals for people living with mental health problems: a systematic review and narrative synthesis of the evidence.' *BMC Psychiatry*, 18, 31.

gratitude to animals you see in fields and farms that are giving their lives for you. If you can, try to purchase free-range products and avoid meats from animals farmed in horrific conditions.

You can also 'adopt' an animal by spending a small amount each month on its upkeep to help care for it in a shelter, a sanctuary or a natural setting. If you decide to get a pet, go to a rescue centre and give an abandoned or neglected animal a loving home. Animal-rescue centres also welcome volunteers or gifts of animal food. And then there are charities that you can support that raise money to prevent animal cruelty. Become a good Samaritan for animals as well as humans. In my opinion, a kind world is one where animals are treated kindly.

Nature – Way 88: Save a spider

What's your instinctive reaction when you see a spider? I bet it's to scream, and ask someone else to deal with it, or perhaps kill it. It's a natural reaction, as spiders have long skinny legs, look sinister and move really fast. They weave their webs to capture unsuspecting victims. These creepy crawlies may also bite, and some can prove deadly. But this way to be kinder to nature asks you to follow the advice of entomologists (insect experts[159]) and save a spider, rather than scream about it. Let me explain why.

First of all, spiders are a living part of nature and an indoor ecosystem. And most of them are not aggressive or dangerous, just secretive. The spiders that bite aren't typically the ones that come into our homes and, even if they do bite, their venom is mostly so weak it does little harm to humans. Also, it's not easy for a spider to bite you and they are unlikely to do so as they are far more afraid of you than you are of them. But, most important of all, contrary to what you may believe, spiders don't harm our

---

159 https://home.howstuffworks.com/green-living/dont-kill-spiders.htm.

homes. They actually help us by capturing and eating disease-ridden insects, bugs and pests without us having to use chemicals to do so. Daddy long-legs do the same – they capture mosquitoes.

It's the same with bees and wasps. It's frightening when these buzzing bugs get trapped in our homes. We all fear their sting, but bees and wasps also provide a service for us. They pollinate flowers and are important for the production of seeds and the fruit needed for our food chain, not to mention honey. An estimated 300,000 plants need those pollinators. Sadly, the number of bees is declining fast, so we need to save, not kill our bees.

Take action

Granted that having spiders around your home may not be pleasant but, if you can, just let them keep your home pest-free. Even if you don't see them, they are always around, sharing your home anyway. If, however, you really want a spider out of your home, don't try to kill it. Instead place a cup or glass over it. Slide a piece of paper underneath and then take it outside where it can carry on its life somewhere else, as spiders live happily outside as well as indoors.

It's the same with bees and wasps. Stay calm when you see them. Screaming and making sudden movements just alarms them and makes them more likely to sting you. Open the window and let them find their own way out. They just want to get outside and carry on with their busy lives. Wasps are less attractive than bees and you are more likely to want to kill or swat them. But, when you kill a wasp, it omits a chemical that alerts other wasps, so you could be making more trouble for yourself. So, if you can, just leave them alone!

Nature – Way 89: Appreciate birds

Birds are as important as other animals, insects and plants for maintaining a healthy ecological balance, so we should be kind to them. They can also provide moments of enchantment. If you have ever woken up early to hear the dawn chorus, you will know how blissful it sounds. The music of nature is captivating and fosters your connection to the natural world. Birdsong is also very calming, and research[160] confirms that listening to birdsong can promote both relaxation and increased concentration. So, this way to be kinder to nature not only encourages you to listen more attentively to birdsong, but also to do some birdwatching.

As birdwatching requires mindful attention, it can boost mood and health. It encourages you to observe the natural world in absolute silence, and helps you tune into your own state of mind and feel more compassionate towards yourself and the great outdoors. The more birdwatching you do, the calmer you are likely to feel, as it puts everything else in your life into perspective. Indeed, one expert[161] states that observing birds shows great promise in preventative healthcare and can make urban areas healthier and happier places to live.

Take action

Whenever you get a chance, step outside and listen to the dawn chorus or the birds singing. If it isn't possible to go outside, the good news[162] is that listening to recordings of birdsong can be just as therapeutic, so make this part of your relaxation routine.

The ideal time to watch birds is mid-afternoon. Simply head into your garden or a local park and find somewhere quiet. If you have binoculars, bring them along, but they are not essential. Focus

---

160 University of Exeter (2017) 'Watching birds near your home is good for your mental health.' ScienceDaily, 25 February 2017.

161 Cox, D. University of Exeter: www.exeter.ac.uk/news/featurednews/title_571299_en.html.

162 Gould van Praag, C.D. *et al.* (2017) 'Mind-wandering and alterations to default mode network connectivity when listening to naturalistic versus artificial sounds.' *Scientific Reports*, 7, 45273.

your attention on the activity of the birds around you – it doesn't matter what species you see, it's your observation of them and how they help you feel more connected to nature that's important.

Be as silent as you can. Don't offer the birds food or try to get them to come close, just watch them. Lose yourself in watching them. Then, when you are ready to leave, give thanks to the birds for the connection to nature they have given you.

If you feel anxious around birds, try watching butterflies or ants instead. The therapeutic impact is similar.

You may find that birdwatching becomes addictive and you wish to do something to help them. If you have a garden, hang up a bird feeder, but make sure it is squirrel-proof. You can also join a local birdwatching group as well as bird-protection societies, and use bird-counting apps to help wildlife experts track and safeguard bird populations.

Nature – Way 90: Go with the flow

Water gives life and, through water, we are all connected to nature and to life itself. You may find that you instinctively feel drawn to water, lakes, rivers, seas and oceans. In ancient times, communities that lived close to water sources were more likely to survive because water sustained them. Water is the most essential natural force on Earth and without it you couldn't live. Your body consists of up to 70 per cent water and it also takes up around 70 per cent of the planet. In essence, water is nature. That's why this way to be kinder to nature encourages you to get closer to water, both emotionally and physically.

Studies[163] show that being close to water can boost mood, concentration and induce feelings of calm. Seeing the natural

---

163 www.nbcnews.com/better/health/what-beach-does-your-brain-ncna787231.

beauty of rivers, waterfalls, lakes and oceans also promotes awe and a sense of connection to something bigger than yourself. The 'blue mind' ethos is all about the healing power of water and is supported by increasing numbers of scientists,[164] with some even believing that spending time close to water may one day be recommended by doctors for its medicinal benefits.

Take action

To help you connect to water, try to visit a waterside location as often as you can. It can be the sea or a river or a lake. It doesn't matter which, as long as there is open water. When you are there, watch the water flowing or the waves dancing and let your thoughts merge with them. Water can heal and be a teacher. What is it reflecting to you? During your waterside walks, if you notice any litter, become a water warrior and pick it up to dispose of safely. Be sure to wear protective gloves. There are also waterside litter collection groups you can offer your services to.

If it isn't possible to visit a waterside location, you can listen to the sound of water on a recording online or via an app. Or you can bring a water feature into your home or even install a fish tank – watching fish swim has a therapeutic effect.

You can also connect with nature by giving wild swimming in open water a try. This has become very popular in recent years, but be sure to take precautions and stay safe, as hidden currents and debris can be dangerous. Swim parallel to the shore, preferably with companions, and at supervised locations where lifeguards are on duty.

And with your newfound sense of reconnection and respect for water, start actively valuing and conserving it. Small things

---

164 Gascon, M. *et al.* (2017) 'Outdoor blue spaces, human health and well-being: A systematic review of quantitative studies.' *International Journal of Hygiene and Environmental Health*, 220(8) 1207–1221.

can make a big difference. Turn off the tap while brushing your teeth, shower instead of taking a bath. And stop drinking bottled water – filter your tap water instead. You will save money and help save the planet by reducing plastic waste.

Nature – Way 91: Become a litter warrior

The previous ten ways to be kinder to nature encouraged you to feel more connected to nature in the hope that this will encourage you to be kinder to our beautiful planet. Mother Earth really is in urgent need of your kindness, with the seas filled with eight million tons of plastic waste that can enter the food chain. In Way 90, I encouraged you to pick up litter while walking beside open water, and this way to be kind takes things one step further by asking you to become a litter warrior every day.

Litter is unpleasant and makes beaches, parks and beautiful scenic spots look untidy but, far worse, it is dangerous. It can trap and make wildlife sick, and poison both the waters and the land. Plastic waste is particularly toxic. One of the kindest things you can do for Mother Earth is to keep her clean and litter-free. You may feel you are fighting a losing battle, but litter experts[165] have shown that people are far less likely to litter an area if they find it clean or see someone, like you, picking up litter.

An added bonus is that research[166] has also suggested that taking part in litter pick-up campaigns is not just good for the planet, but also a rewarding experience for the volunteers.

---

165 www.theatlantic.com/health/archive/2014/08/littering-and-following-the-crowd/374913.

166 Wyles, K.J. *et al.* (2017) 'Can beach cleans do more than clean-up litter? Comparing beach cleans to other coastal activities.' *Environment and Behavior*, 49(5) 509–535.

Take action

You can volunteer to become part of a group devoted to keeping a specific area of natural beauty clean, or you can simply pick up litter independently whenever you can and dispose of it safely. You may even want to combine picking up litter with exercise. In Sweden, this is called *plogging* – jogging or brisk walking as you pick up litter.

It's important to say safe when picking up litter, so carry protective gloves with you to keep your hands away from anything harmful. If there are plenty of waste bins in the area, put the litter in them but, if waste bins are scarce, carry a bin bag with you.

If you notice needles or anything potentially dangerous, such as old batteries or chemicals, or any faeces, the golden rule is *not* to pick it up. It's also best to avoid glass objects or anything with sharp edges. If in any doubt, leave it and alert the local authorities, council or landowner, so they can dispose of it. Report any dead animals you see too.

If you feel inspired, you may want to see if the litter you collect can be recycled, but whether you decide to do that or not, even picking up one item every day is playing your part in making the world a cleaner, tidier and healthier place. And, lastly, even though you will have been wearing gloves while picking up litter, always wash your hands thoroughly afterwards.

Nature – Way 92: Reduce your plastic footprint

There is a plastic crisis in the world today. Plastic causes massive environmental problems[167] and is having a fatal impact on nature. It releases toxic chemicals that, when ingested, can kill wildlife and animals, especially fish. What makes plastic such a

---

167 www.nationalgeographic.com/magazine/2018/06/plastic-planet-animals-wildlife-impact-waste-pollution.

deadly enemy is that it is virtually impossible to destroy. Once it is out there in the environment, it doesn't disintegrate – it just lingers on for up to a thousand years, causing more and more damage. One way to be kind to yourself and others, and to help protect the natural resources for future generations, is to cut down on the amount of plastic in your life and the lives of others. Of course, governments, businesses and authorities need to lead the way but there are many everyday things you can do to reduce your plastic footprint.

Take action

We buy and discard millions of single-use water bottles every single day. A great way to start cutting down on your plastic use is to use a refillable bottle. It's the same with coffee and tea takeaway cups – carry a reusable cup with you. Most coffee houses these days sell them, even offering a discount on your coffee if you use one.

The next step is to monitor your use of straws. Do you really need one? If you are buying a drink, ask the server not to add a straw unless absolutely essential. And if you do need to use a straw, carry a reusable one. Avoid plastic cutlery whenever you can, too. Take a spoon and fork with you if you know you are going to need them.

Whenever you go shopping in a supermarket, get into the habit of taking reusable bags with you. Most supermarkets these days sell them. If you find it hard to remember bags, purchase a fold-away one that you can carry in your pocket or bag. And while on the subject of food, buying in bulk helps cut down on the amount of plastic packaging.

Microbeads have largely been banned but do make sure you avoid anything that contains any of the following environmental toxins: polyethylene (PE), polypropylene (PP), polyethylene terephthalate (PET), polymethyl methacrylate (PMMA), polytetrafluoroethylene (PTFE) and nylon.

Giving up chewing gum is also helpful, as it's made from synthetic rubber, a type of plastic. As far as detergents are concerned, purchase those in cardboard boxes rather than bottles. Use matches instead of lighters and buy fresh food rather than frozen, which tends to be packaged in plastic. If possible, aim to buy produce in boxes rather than in any kind of packaging.

If you have children, you may want to consider cloth rather than disposable nappies (diapers). Razors with replaceable blades are more environmentally friendly than disposable ones.

Even making these small changes can have a positive impact on reducing your plastic footprint. Once you become fully aware of just how much plastic there is in your life and how unkind plastic is to the planet, you will be eager to make these small changes and help free the world from the curse of plastic.

Nature – Way 93: Use it again

If you want to make a real difference with your life and help save the planet, make recycling your mantra. It may feel inconvenient at first, a fiddly and messy waste of precious time – sorting out bottles and plastics and so on into separate recycling bins – but once you fully understand[168] the reasons for what you are doing, you will know what a positive difference recycling can make.

Every time you recycle or re-use something you would have normally thrown away, you are conserving the world's resources, because used materials are transformed into new products and there is no need to plunder natural resources. If you don't recycle

---

168 Chase, N. *et al.* (2009) '"This is public health: Recycling counts!" Description of a pilot health communications campaign.' *International Journal of Environmental Research and Public Health*, 6(12) 2980–2991.

old products, new resources are utilised through farming, mining or forestry. Recycling doesn't just protect resources, it also helps protect natural habitats.

Recycling saves energy, because it requires far less energy than processing raw products. Recycling reduces the need for extracting and refining, and therefore cuts down on air and water pollution. It also reduces unhealthy greenhouse gas emissions. Last, but by no means least, recycling reduces landfill – the rubbish we send to sites – which produces unwanted greenhouse gas emissions, such as methane.

There is a lot of confusion about how to recycle, but this way to be kind offers some easy guidelines.

Take action

For the best ways to cut down on plastic use, refer back to the previous way to be kind (Way 92), and aim to recycle all plastic that you do use.

Save trees and forests by cutting down on the amount of paper you use. If you can, send an email or a text rather than a card or a letter and if you don't need printed documents and can work online, aim to do so. If you have to use paper, use both sides. And whenever you want to discard paper, magazines, newspapers and books, put them in the recycling bin. Recycling one ton of paper can save around fifteen trees, thousands of gallons of water and three cubic yards of landfill space.

And be sure to send your old mobile phones, laptops and PCs to either be recycled or used by someone else less fortunate than you, whenever you upgrade. Such waste contributes massively to unnecessary landfill waste. And recycle your batteries and empty ink and toner cartridges too. When buying new products, choose those you know can be recycled, as well as products that have already been recycled.

Above all, ensure that you have recycling bins readily available in your home and workspace for paper, plastic, cloth and metal. Label them appropriately. Sometimes the difference between recycling something or not comes down to convenience. Make recycling part of your life and as easy to do as possible. To ensure that you are recycling the right things in the right way, check out your local area's recycling guide.

Nature – Way 94: Stretch your legs

It took the pandemic lockdowns of 2020 to offer us a glimpse of life with less traffic on the roads and in the skies. Pictures of wild animals reclaiming the roads circulated online, gathering a great deal of positive attention. My readers sent me beautiful pictures of clear skies, having spotted reassuring shapes, in particular clouds taking the shape of angel wings. I live fairly close to a major airport and the silence above was very much welcomed as I wrote my books. I could hear the birds singing without interruption from the whirling of engines. But not only was the peace extremely calming and therapeutic, research[169] showed that it significantly reduced air pollution, caused by CO_2 emissions from cars, buses, taxis and planes.

This way to be kind encourages you to use the clear roads and clear-sky inspiration of the lockdowns and continue to play your part in helping reduce air pollution by walking more and driving less. And if the distance is too great to walk, then cycle, use public transport or consider the option of car-sharing. Of course, there are always going to be times when you really do need to drive but, whenever possible, stretch your legs rather than reach for your car

---

169 Bao, R. *et al.* (2020) 'Does lockdown reduce air pollution? Evidence from 44 cities in northern China.' *Science of The Total Environment*, 731, 139052.

keys. An added bonus is your increased health and fitness as, even in urban areas where air pollution is likely to be high, research[170] has shown that the fitness benefits far outweigh any harmful effects of air pollution.

Take action

Commit to giving your car more breaks and your feet more work-outs. If you don't think you have enough time, all it requires is some forward planning, especially when the car journey is short. Remind yourself that walking is a simple way to get much-need-ed exercise without the sweat of going to the gym. It also saves money on parking and petrol and is completely free. You will be getting all the health benefits of fresh air and daylight, and some downtime to reflect and gather your thoughts.

Surprisingly, walking – especially if you live in a city – may be quicker than driving. We often forget how much time we spend in traffic, as well as unexpected roadworks or other delays, such as filling up with petrol and finding a convenient parking spot. And perhaps most important of all, walking instead of driving helps the planet.

You may also want to reassess the amount of air travel you undertake, as frequent flying is another major cause of air pol-lution. It took the pandemic travel restrictions to force many of us to consider whether or not we really needed to drive or fly to meetings, or if online communication would suffice. It also made us consider holidaying closer to home. Obviously, personal interaction is of great value but, before you drive or fly anywhere, think carefully if it is really necessary.

---

170 www.newscientist.com/article/2087059-walking-and-cycling-are-still-good-for-you-despite-air-pollution.

Nature – Way 95: Meat first

As I am an animal lover, my decision to become a vegetarian was a no-brainer. I've not eaten meat since I was a young child and have never regretted it. I've never had serious health or weight issues and I do wonder if my meat-free life plays a part in that. However, I'm not the kind of person to force my food choices on others, and I respect that everyone should make up their own mind about what suits them best. Indeed, neither of my children are vegetarian. However, what I cannot abide is animal cruelty and mistreatment of any kind and sadly the world is awash with it. In a kind world, living creatures are treated humanely. Indigenous cultures eat meat but they have respect and reverence for the life the animal has sacrificed. It would be a wonderful step towards a kinder world if respect for livestock and their wellbeing before slaughter had a higher priority.

This way to be kind encourages you to either avoid meat or at least cut down on it because a diet rich in meat is associated with an increased risk of obesity and poor health.[171] You don't need meat to get essential proteins – you can get the same health benefits from eggs, fish, nuts and plant-based produce. Eating less meat is not just kinder to your digestion system though, it may be one of the kindest things you can do for the planet. Research[172] has shown that although eating some kinds of meat, in particular red meat, is unhealthier for us than others, farming livestock is more harmful to the living world than growing plant protein. Farming animals utilises around 80 per cent of the world's agricultural land but delivers under 20 per cent of our calories. A plant-based diet therefore cuts the use of land significantly and by so doing halves the greenhouse gases and other pollution caused by food production.

Pause for thought for meat lovers everywhere!

---

171 www.health.harvard.edu/staying-healthy/whats-the-beef-with-red-meat.

172 Poore, J. *et al.* (2018) 'Reducing food's environmental impacts through producers and consumers.' *Science*, 360(6392) 987–992.

Take action

If you already avoid meat, know that you are playing your part in saving nature. If you do eat meat, make thinking about how much meat you eat each day your first priority. Think of ways to cut down. The best way to start cutting own on meat is to eliminate processed meats you consume, such as sausages and bacon. Then consider your choice of red meat. Beef is one of the most toxic to the planet to produce and may contribute up to 35 per cent of all food-related greenhouse gas emissions. Start substituting meat with more fish or poultry instead.

As well as cutting down the amount of times you consume red meat to perhaps once or twice a week, you can also consider cutting down your portion size. Eat less meat and add more healthy options such as vegetables and grains. And prioritise plant-based foods at all times.

Nature – Way 96: Switch off

Recently, I was listening to the radio and heard a radio host asking his guest about ageing and the feeling that he was becoming more like his parents. The guest laughed and said he knew he had left his youth behind when he realised he was regularly reprimanding his teenage children for forgetting to switch off lights.

Switching off lights and appliances does feel like a grown-up, responsible thing to do and is cost effective, too, as you save money over time. It is also the right thing to do for the planet. It's a simple and extremely effective way to conserve energy. There is a direct connection between your energy usage in your home, workplace and the environment, with research[173] even suggesting

---

173 Abel, D.W. *et al.* (2019) 'Air quality-related health benefits of energy efficiency in the United States.' *Environmental Science & Technology*, 53(7) 3987–3998.

that the more we turn off our lights, the more lives we save. You see, the less energy you use at home and work, the fewer power plant emissions are caused to generate electricity, and this helps conserve the Earth's natural resources.

Take action

Enjoy the responsible feeling that washes over you every time you switch off a light when you leave a room or find one that doesn't need to be on. And be sure to switch your light bulbs to low-energy LED energy-efficient ones. They use considerably less energy and last much longer.

Looking ahead, extend being responsible to appliances. Don't leave them on standby, switch them off. If you can, wash your clothes with warm or cold, not hot, water in the washing machine, and hang wet clothes out on a washing line outside to dry. When cooking, open the windows instead of using an extractor fan. Use your dishwasher less often and revert to good, old-fashioned hand-washing of dishes. You can have some great conversations after dinner while one of you washes and the other dries the dishes. Showering, rather than bathing, saves water and is more hygienic. Set your water heater to the lowest comfortable temperature setting.

Insulating your home can also help you conserve energy and save money on central heating. Close doors to keep the heat in when it's cold outside and invest in smart thermostats that can be programmed remotely from your phone and can easily adjust to your preferences without you having to do anything.

Leaving a computer monitor on is something many of us are likely do and is only a small drain on energy but, if numerous appliances are running at the same time, this can all add up. The best advice is to save your work and power down your technology devices when you are not using them.

You may also want to invest in energy-efficient appliances for your home and consider switching to a green energy supplier offering renewable energy generated from windmills and solar panels or green gas produced by breaking down organic manure and sewage.

A greener home is a kinder home.

Nature – Way 97: Go wild

An immediate, effective and extremely positive way to connect better with nature and help the planet is to opt for organic products wherever possible. This reduces animal cruelty and the levels of pesticides, artificial fertilisers and herbicides that are poisoning our natural resources. Doing this also significantly promotes environmentally sustainable management of the land, nature and wildlife by reducing soil erosion and conserving water. Every single time you choose organic food, drink or any kind of organic produce you are being kinder to nature.

Whenever you eat organic products you are not just reducing your own risk of ingesting harmful, non-environmentally friendly toxins and boosting your health and wellbeing, you are also, according to some experts,[174] helping to save the planet. And don't just stop with your food; consider the organic option whenever it is available with the products that you buy and then take this closer-to-nature ethos into all areas of your life.

Take action

While it is true that organic produce can be slightly more expensive than non-organic produce, it is a choice you can make. If you really can't afford to go fully organic, try to ensure that the foods you

---

174 https://time.com/4871915/health-benefits-organic-food.

eat daily – for example, eggs, fruit, vegetables and meats – are fresh and, as a rule of thumb, be wary of buying foods that typically have a high pesticide count, in particular strawberries, spinach, kale, nectarines, apples, grapes, peaches, cherries, pears, tomatoes, celery and potatoes. If you buy these foods, try to buy organic versions.

Be aware that for a food to be genuinely organic it either needs to have United States Department of Agriculture (USDA)-approved[175] or UK government-approved organic control bodies, and don't be deceived by healthy-sounding words like 'natural' or 'made with real fruit' or 'reduced sugar' when buying packaged foods. You need to make sure your organic food has been checked for authenticity by a trusted source. If in doubt, ask the supermarket, farm or shop where you are buying your food to clarify.

However, it's not just organic food that you should seek out. Use organic beauty treatments and household cleaning products too, and organic treatments in your own garden. Buy clothes made from natural organic fibres. There are so many organic options these days to choose from.

Once you start including more organic food in your diet, you will notice a difference in your eating preferences. Your taste buds will get used to the additive-free taste of real food and the thought of packaged, processed and refined foods will lose its appeal. A fast-food take-away option may even make you feel slightly sick. That's a good sign and means that your digestive system is craving natural food sources. It's also a sign that you are becoming wilder at heart. Celebrate your back-to-Earth instinct by spending more and more time in woods, parks and beaches. Join nature protection societies and support conservation projects. Feed the birds. Adopt a wild animal.

Become wilder and closer to nature in body, mind and heart.

---

175 www.ams.usda.gov/sites/default/files/media/Labeling%20Organic%20
   Products.pdf.

Nature – Way 98: Rethink your 'stuff'

The advent of online shopping means that we live in a world where shops never close and you can literally shop all day, every day. The 2020 pandemic may have put the future of high-street shopping at risk, but it gave a huge boost to online retailers, with virtual sales scaling the heights. This trend looks set to continue. There is no doubt that we live in a material world and we surround ourselves with material things. What we spend our hard-earned money on is our own choice and we all deserve to treat ourselves and our loved ones. But the pandemic may have turned the spotlight on your spending habits. How much of what you are buying do you really need?

This way to be kinder to the world and to protect its natural resources encourages you to think about all the 'stuff' in your life. If your house was flooded, what items would you rescue first? The chances are it would be things of sentimental value because they remind you of loved ones or happy times. The old cliché – you can't take it with you – really is true. Most of us shop more than we need to and have far too much 'stuff' in our lives. Over-consumption not only pollutes the planet, it is a recognised cause[176] of stress, anxiety and depression.

Take action

For the next ten days, set yourself this challenge. Every time you get an urge to visit Amazon or any other online retailer to purchase an item, put it in the 'buy later' basket and tell yourself that if you still want it in ten days' time, you can always buy it then. Then, write down the cost of the item in a notebook.

---

176 Vartanian, L.R. *et al.* (2016) 'Clutter, chaos, and overconsumption: The role of mind-set in stressful and chaotic food environments.' *Environment and Behavior*, 49(2) 215–223.

When the ten-day period is up, take a look at your notebook and add up the total cost of the items listed there. Then, instead of spending that money on 'stuff', donate it to a good cause or, if you feel you deserve a treat, spend it on doing something you enjoy, such as a day out. Make sure that what you do is action- not consumer-based. The whole point of this exercise is to encourage you to re-evaluate your spending choices. Sure, some of the items you set aside may be ones you do need, but there will also be items in the basket that are spur-of-the-moment purchases that won't enhance your life but clutter it up and eventually be destined for the already overloaded landfill sites.

Minimalism is a lifestyle choice that offers surprising wellbeing benefits and is much kinder to the planet. It means you having much less 'stuff' but more experiences in your life. It means less having and doing more. It can help create a deeper and more meaningful life and a better, more natural world.

Nature – Way 99: Inspire those who will follow in your footsteps

You will be a role model for future generations. Children and teenagers, whether they realise it or not, look to those older than them for guidance and inspiration. So, one way you can help make the world a kinder place is to teach by your example. And this is especially the case when it comes to the natural world. Show children a better way. The future is theirs to create and you can play a part in helping them to understand the importance of being kind to the natural world. Research[177] shows that educating children to respect nature is key.

---

177 Veselinovska, S.S. *et al.* (2010) 'How to help children understand and respect nature?' *Procedia Social and Behavioral Sciences*, 2 (2010) 2244–2247.

Take action

If you are a parent or a grandparent, teach children to connect to nature and wildlife with gratitude. The sooner you start, the better, as young minds are so receptive. If you are playing with a toddler and see a spider, tell the child that spiders are our friends and discuss how busy and productive their lives are. Whenever you are outside, if you see a rainbow, a beautiful sunset or fascinating shapes in the clouds, take a few moments to stop and look at them in awe. Encourage your children to respect the natural places they visit, such as parks and beaches. Tell them how litter is really dangerous to wildlife and explain how you can help clean it up (Way 91).

Allow children to experience nature. Ensure that they are safe but let them walk barefoot on the grass or sand. Allow them to play with mud, climb trees and smell flowers. Let them plant bulbs in a pot and give them the responsibility of taking care of that plant. Get them to help you put up a bird feeder in your garden. If you visit the beach, go shell-hunting and tell them if they hold a shell to their ear, they might be able to hear the sea whispering to them. Keep exposing them to the great outdoors as much as possible, to encourage that special bond with nature. And keep explaining to them why Mother Nature needs them to help protect her and why you are saving water, switching off lights, sorting out rubbish for recycling.

Don't underestimate the impact of nature documentaries, books and videos to encourage children to bond with nature but, above all, don't undervalue your own reaction to nature – your children will pick up on your love for it and emulate you.

If you are not a parent, your role as an eco-guardian is just as important because the younger generation needs you to show them the way. Take small steps each day to help make the planet a cleaner, safer and less toxic place. Set the best example you can for the next generation who hold the future wellbeing of the planet in their tiny hands.

Nature – Way 100: Choose to be kind

We have seen throughout this book how simple, everyday actions can make a big difference,[178] not just to our own quality of life but to the lives of others and the planet. A single act of kindness to others has a proven[179] ripple effect. It can make you feel good,[180] and the person who receives it feel good and therefore more likely to be kind to others. So, who knows what chain of kindness you might be setting in motion whenever you do or say something kind?

Being a kind person is a choice you can always make. Although the world may sometimes drag you down, it can never take away your freedom of choice, your choice to be kind.

To give you an immediate example, if this book has changed your life for the better, you now have a choice about what to do with it, once you've read the brief conclusion that follows and explored the Resources. You can keep it to yourself or you can choose to incorporate the suggestions into your life and also share what you have discovered with others. This applies not just to what you have learned but to the actual book itself. If you have a hard copy, you can give it as a gift to someone you know or leave it in a public place for someone randomly to find. And if you own a digital version of this book, you may want to send it as a gift to someone to help spread the word and save a few trees in the process.

Take action

Now is the time to make the compassionate choice to be kind in your daily life. Granted, this isn't going to solve the world's

---

178 www.health.harvard.edu/blog/the-heart-and-science-of-kindness-2019041816447.

179 www.scientificamerican.com/article/kindness-contagion.

180 Rowland, L. *et al.* (2019) 'A range of kindness activities boost happiness.' *Journal of Social Psychology*, 159(3) 340–343.

problems but what it can do is bring hope that positive change is possible. Your small daily acts of kindness, however tiny they may feel, really do make a difference because collectively they can be the force that ignites positive change.

There's no time to waste. Every morning, you have a brand-new chance to be the difference you want to see in the world, so take it. By so doing you are helping create a gentler, more inclusive and environmentally friendly world. Practise each day with Aesop's wise words, 'No act of kindness is ever wasted' as your guiding mantra.

Remember, every word or act of kindness increases not just the self-esteem and happiness of the recipient but your happiness, too. It's a winning choice for you, for everyone you interact with on a daily basis and for the entire planet.

The world urgently needs you to choose and share your kindness everywhere you go, and light the way ahead following the devastation the pandemic heaped on humanity. So, become a walking inspiration right now, and show others through your words and actions just how joyful and enhancing a life centred around kindness can be.

CHAPTER 6

CONCLUSION: KIND HEARTS

I've been searching for ways to heal and I've found that kindness is the best way. Lady Gaga

Congratulations for reading to this point and finding the courage to be kind. Every kind person is a unique individual but, one thing they have in common is that they are all brave hearts. The heart is an organ and, contrary to what you may think, it gets stronger the more you feel and use it. Even broken hearts can grow back wiser and stronger. In 2020, the beating heart of the planet was broken by the Coronavirus and humanity plunged into grief, loss and crisis not seen for decades. But we also saw the very best of humanity surfacing. We saw kindness, compassion and love rise like a phoenix from the ashes.

During times of crisis and despair, the only way out is to find a sense of meaning and purpose in life and that is perhaps the most powerful reason of all to be kind. Being kind can give you hope that who you are really does matter, a hope that kindness can make a real and lasting difference in the world.

Of course, you aren't always going to be as kind as you could be. I know I am not always the kindest of people. I am a human being and human beings are flawed, but to always be kind remains a goal of mine, an aspiration and an inspiration. I know where I need to be headed and, if we can all share that goal, that aspiration towards kindness, just think what a connected, compassionate and joyful world we can all create together.

An exercise I often ask people to do when they lack meaning and purpose in life is to write their own short obituary. This sounds morbid but the reason I ask them to do this is because it has a way of focusing their attention absolutely on their values and what really matters to them. Why not try it yourself? I have done this exercise many times over the decades and the details vary each time but, the older I get, the shorter my 'obituary' becomes. I list fewer and fewer so-called achievements, awards, publications, and so on. I know I'm still a work in progress and not quite there yet, but I hope, in time, that I can simply write or conclude with the words, 'She was a kind person.' That would be my greatest accolade of all.

No regrets

When people are close to dying, they don't tend to regret what they did. It is what they *didn't* find the courage to do that they regret the most. Being kind takes a tremendous amount of courage. It is for brave hearts only, but I promise you that if you do live a life of kindness, you will live the best, most fulfilling and happiest life of all – a life of no regrets.

You can always give something, even if it is only kindness.
Anne Frank

YOUR 100 DAYS OF KINDNESS CHALLENGE

For the next 100 days, commit to performing at least one random act of kindness a day, whether that be for yourself, others, the natural world or to help make the world – both off and online – a gentler, better place. At the end of each day, write down your act of kindness so you have a record.

You can follow the 100 ways to be kind in this book or think up your own creative ways to be kind. It doesn't matter how you choose to complete this challenge, just commit to doing at least one act of kindness a day.

It takes time, dedication and courage to be kind. Writing down your acts of kindness will encourage you to be reflective and more likely to make kindness a daily habit, the kind of person you are.

When your 100 days are up, please do get in touch with me and let me know how making kindness your way of life made you feel.

A LETTER FROM THERESA

Thank you for reading *100 Ways to be Kind*. It felt like such an important book to write and I hope with all my heart that it has informed and empowered you to make kindness your daily mantra.

If you did find the book helpful, and want to keep up to date with all my latest releases, just sign up to the following link. Your email address will never be shared and you can unsubscribe at any time:

www.thread-books.com/theresa-cheung

Details about how to get in touch with me if you have any questions to ask or stories to share can be found in the Resources, and if you enjoyed this book, I would be deeply grateful if you could leave a review.

Getting feedback from readers is the reason I keep on writing books. Your feedback also helps to persuade other readers to pick up one of my books, perhaps for the first time. Has this book inspired you? Has it helped? Have the suggestions spoken to you? Has *100 Ways to be Kind* given you pause for thought and encouraged you to treat yourself, others and the planet in a kinder way? If you are new to my writing, I hope you enjoy checking out my previous books and also stay tuned for my upcoming books with Thread.

Thank you again for letting my words speak to you about the life-changing power of kindness.

With love and gratitude, Theresa xx

TheresaCheungAuthor

@theresa_cheung_author

@Theresa_Cheung

www.theresacheung.com

RESOURCES

Recommended reading

The Sensitive Soul by Theresa Cheung (2020, Thread)

Kindness: The Little Thing that Matters Most by Jaime Thurston (2017, Harper Thorsons)

Dare to Be Kind: How Extraordinary Compassion Can Transform Our World by Lizzie Velasquez (2017, Hachette Books)

Kindness: Change Your Life and Make the World a Kinder Place by Gill Hasson (2018, Capstone)

The Year of Surprising Acts of Kindness by Laura Kemp (2018, Orion)

The Little Book of Kindness by Bernadette Russell (2017, Orion)

The Five Side Effects of Kindness by David R. Hamilton (2017, Hay House)

Kindfulness by Padraig O'Morain (2018, Yellow Kite)

Online kindness

Here are some informative, insightful and inspiring online resources that you may find useful.

www.randomactsofkindness.org
Ideas to perform random acts of kindness.

https://cityofkindness.org
Coalition of organisations working to inspire kindness in our world.

www.actionforhappiness.org
Promoting happiness and doing kind things for others.

www.spreadkindness.org
Empowering people to spread kindness around the world.

www.positive.news
https://balance.media
Magazines to promote positive journalism.

www.campaigntoendloneliness.org
Issues surrounding loneliness.

www.kindnessuk.com
Promoting kindness.

www.peopleunited.org.uk
Using art to promote kindness.

www.smallactsofkindness.co.uk
Connecting communities using kindness.

www.kindness.org
Promoting kindness as a catalyst to heal the world.

www.worldanimalprotection.org
Dreaming of a world where animals are free from suffering.

www.greenpeace.org
Campaigning for a future that will allow our oceans and forests to thrive.

ACKNOWLEDGEMENTS

Deepest gratitude to my publisher, Claire Bord, for her vision and guidance and to Kim Nash for her kindness and support and for introducing me to the Thread team. Thanks also to Alexandra Holmes for skillfully guiding the editing and production of this book, to Katherine Mackrill for her copy-editing and to everyone at Thread involved in the production and promotion of this book. I'm also extremely thankful to Ingrid Court-Jones for her invaluable input while I researched and wrote this book.

Sincere thanks to my wise agent Jane Graham Maw (www.grahammawchristie.com) for her patience and support. I am also forever in debt to all my wonderful readers, who are a never-ending source of inspiration to me. Last, but never least, heartfelt thanks to Ray, Robert and Ruthie (and my little dog, Arnie) for their love and support, as I went into self-imposed exile to research and write this book.

ABOUT THE AUTHOR

Sunday Times bestselling author Theresa Cheung has a degree in Theology and English from the University of Cambridge. She has dedicated her writing career to championing the gentle traits of kind and sensitive people and collating their stories. She has also been researching and writing about intuition, dreams, spirituality, holistic wellbeing and personal growth for the last 20 years.

Highly respected by scientists, psychologists and neurologists working in the same field, Theresa has built up a loyal readership and her numerous titles have been translated into dozens of languages. She has an impressive backlist that includes two *Sunday Times* top-ten bestsellers and many books that are consistently top of their categories on Amazon.

Theresa has had her work featured in national magazines and newspapers, including *Grazia*, *Prima*, the *Daily Mail*, the *Sunday Mirror*, the *Daily Express*, the *Sunday Observer* and *The Guardian*, most recently with her latest book *The Premonition Code*. She has been interviewed about being sensitive in an insensitive world by Russell Brand on Episode 71 of his iconic podcast *Under the Skin* and by Piers Morgan on *Good Morning Britain*. She has also appeared on Talkradio, various BBC radio stations, numerous spiritual and popular lifestyle podcasts, such as the award-winning *Lavendaire*, and has also launched her own podcast, *White Shores*.

Theresa's website is: www.theresacheung.com.

Get in touch

The more that kind people share their stories and insights, the stronger and more visible kindness becomes. Please feel free to get in touch with me to share your stories and insights about the power of kindness to change the world for the better, or to ask me questions. I'd love to hear from you. You can subscribe to my newsletter and contact me via my website, www.theresacheung. com. I can also be contacted via my Theresa Cheung Author Facebook, Instagram and Twitter pages or at my reader stories email address: angeltalk710@aol.com. Sometimes, if life gets a little overwhelming, it may take me a while to reply, but know that I intend to reply eventually to everyone who kindly reaches out to me.

CPSIA information can be obtained
at www.ICGtesting.com
Printed in the USA
LVHW041140250920
667084LV00002B/154

9 781800 190917